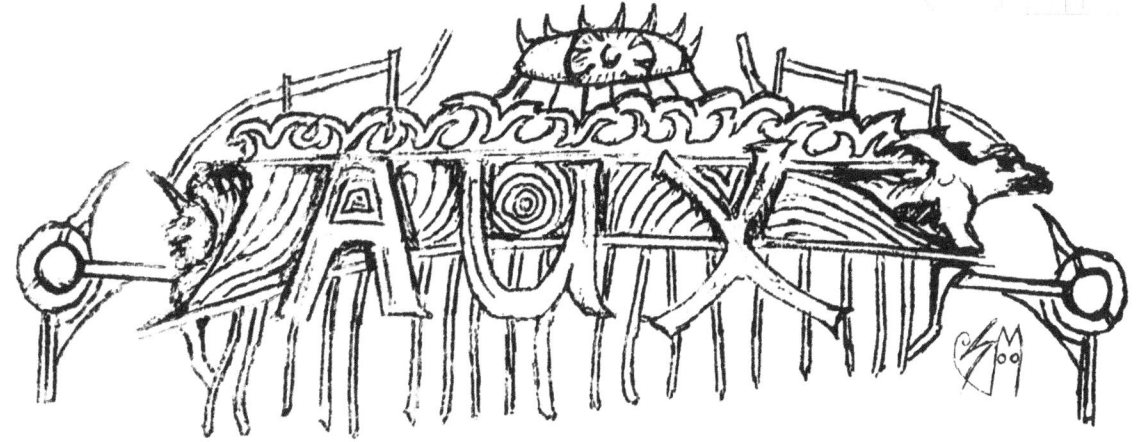

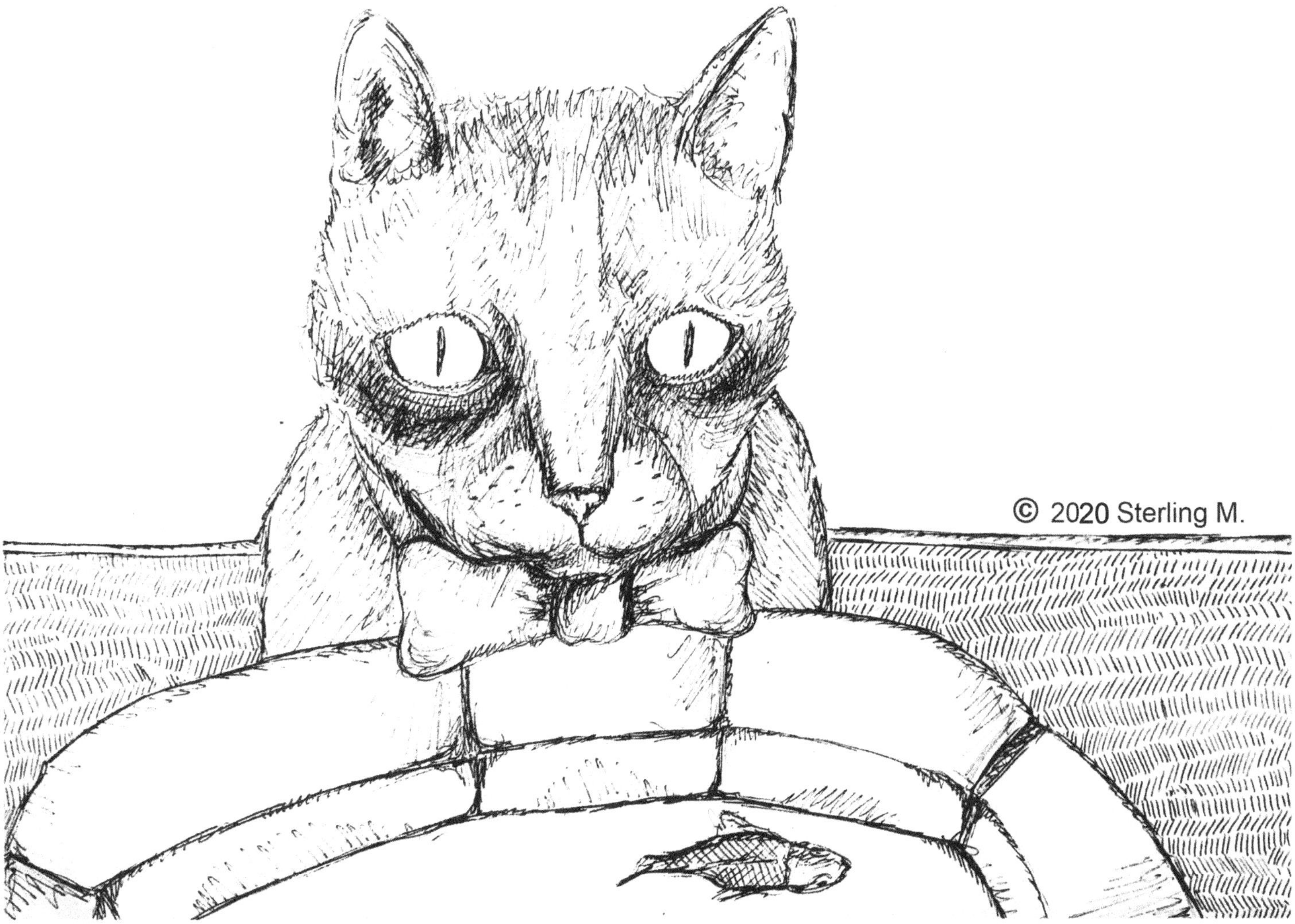

© 2020 Sterling M.

1

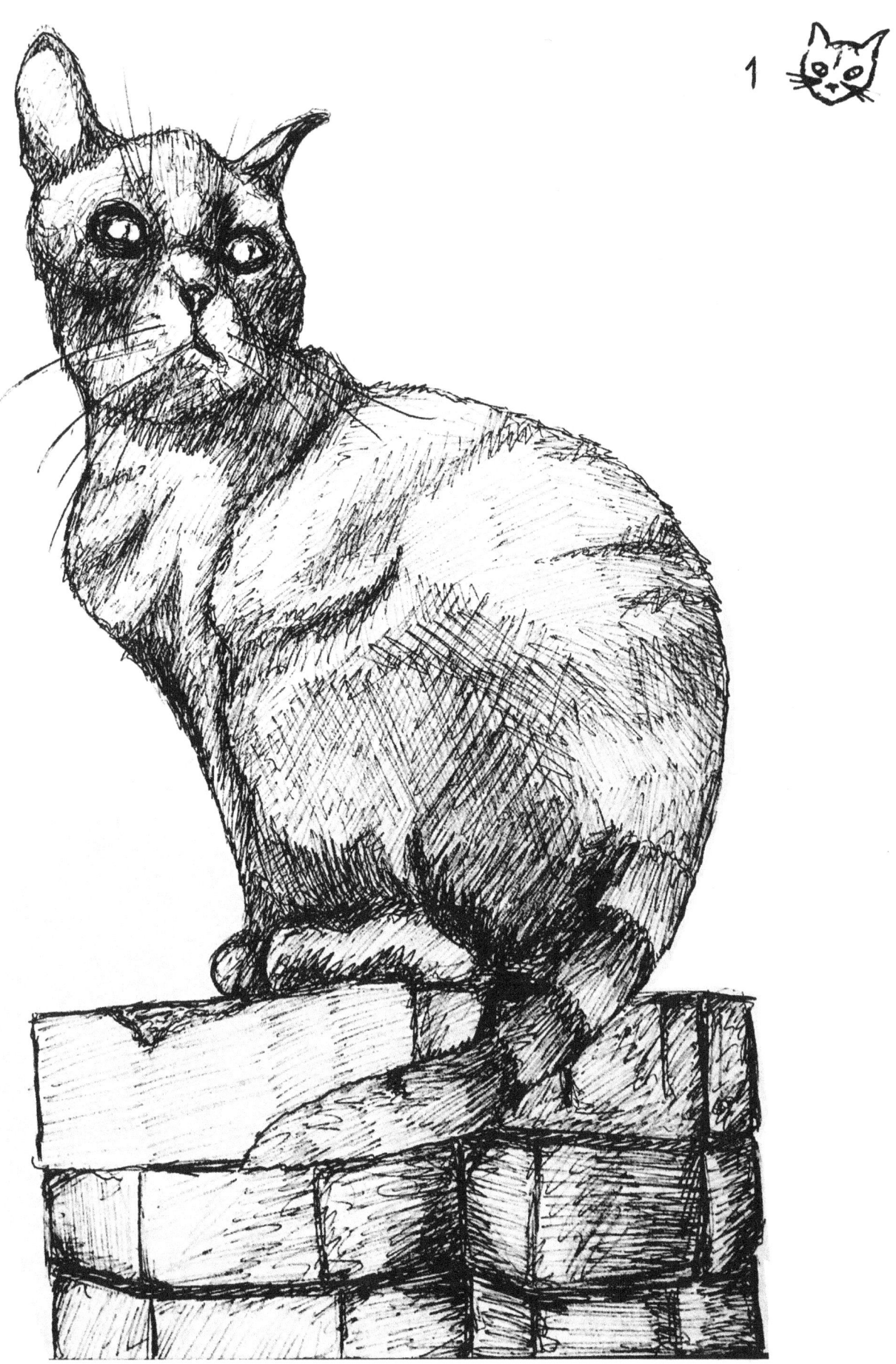

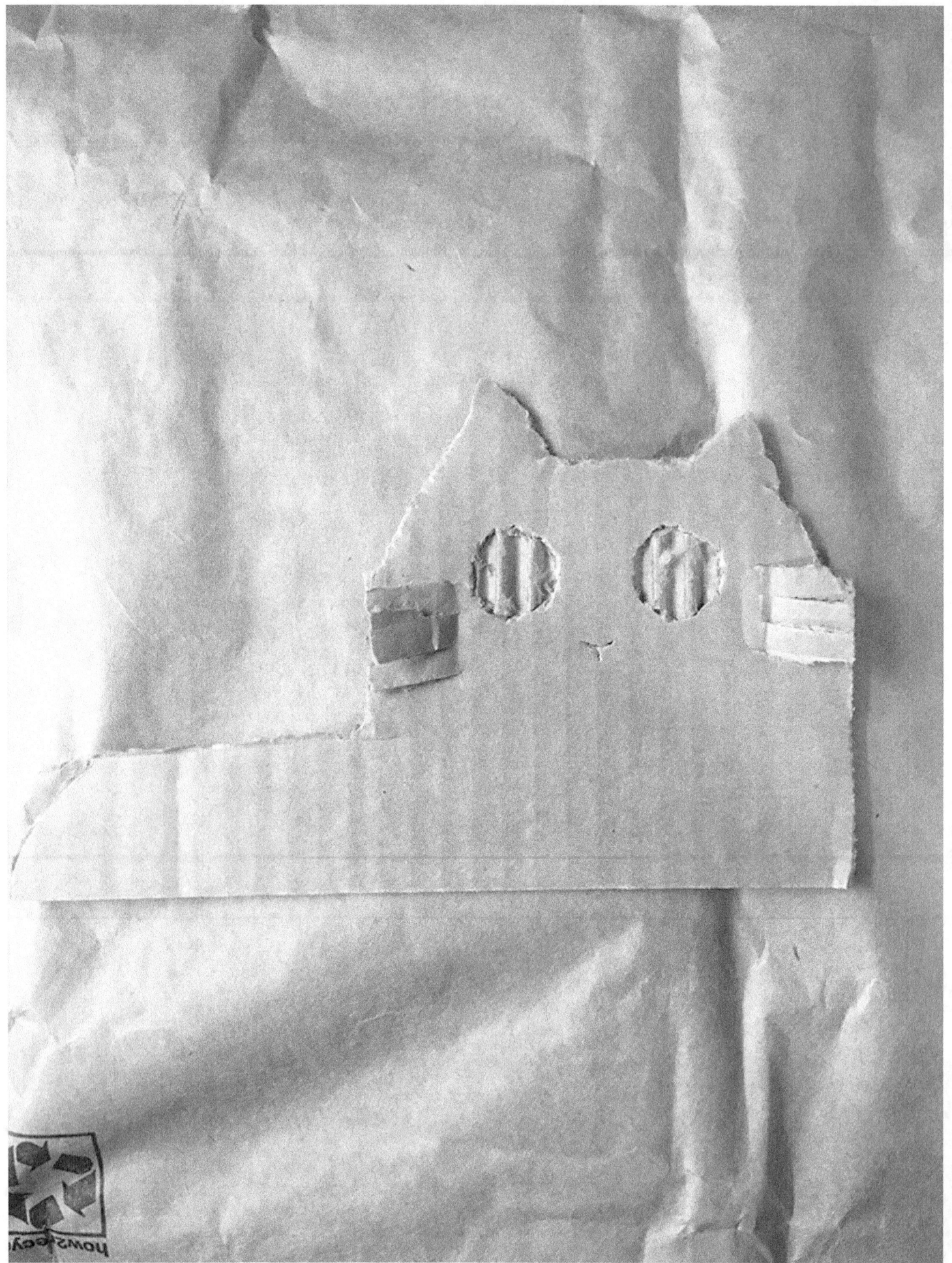

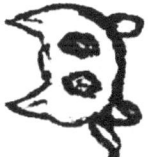

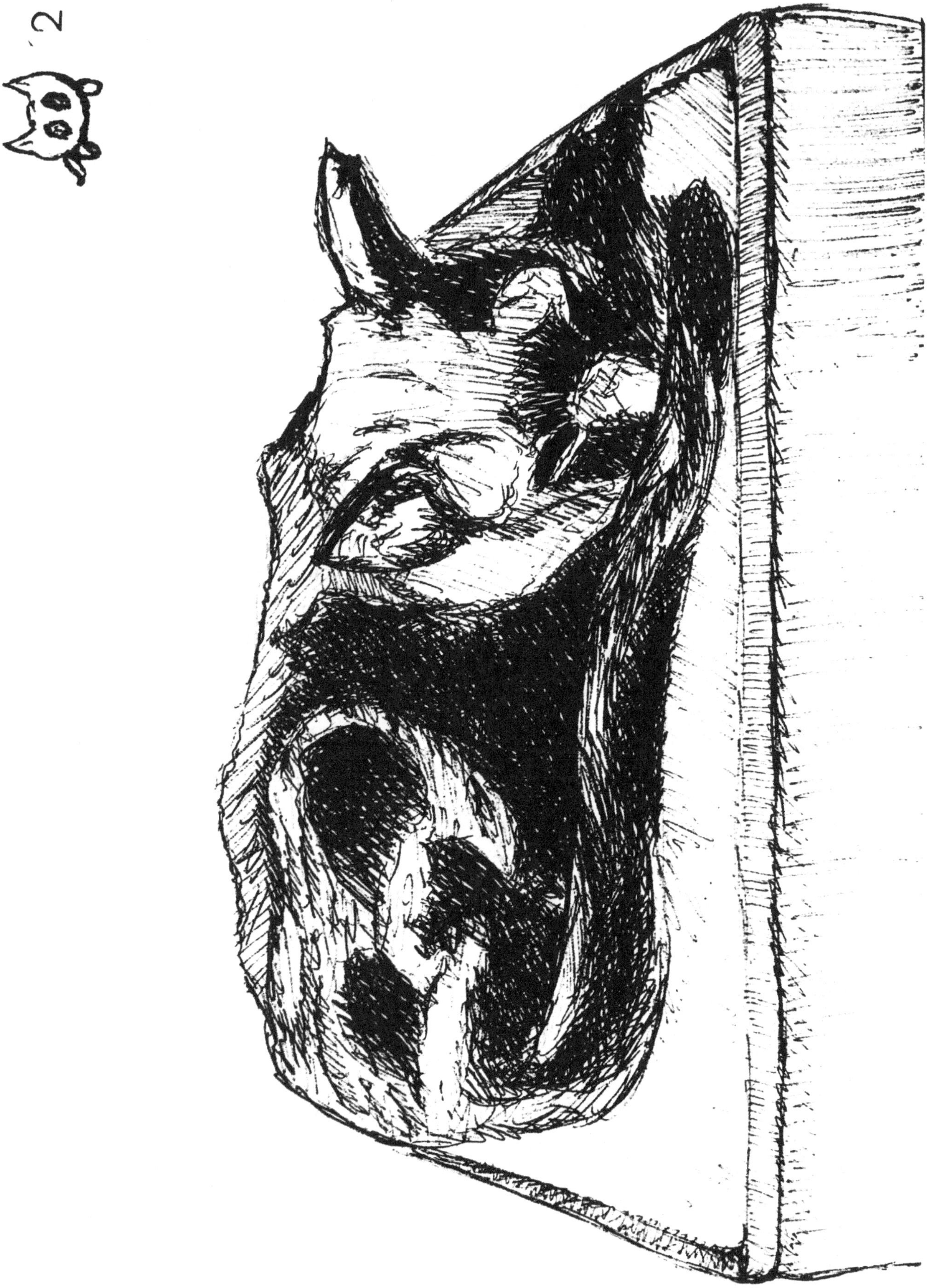

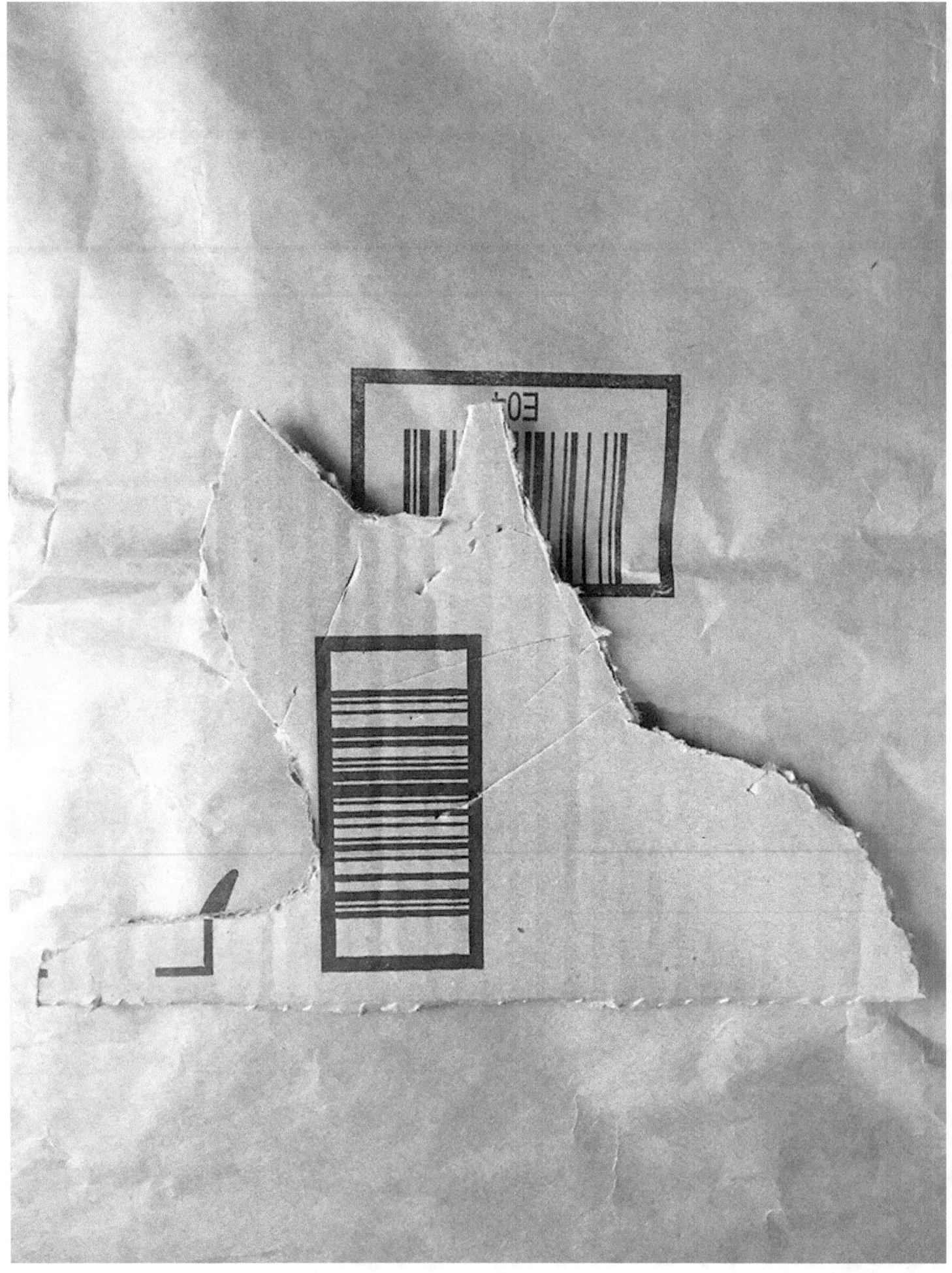

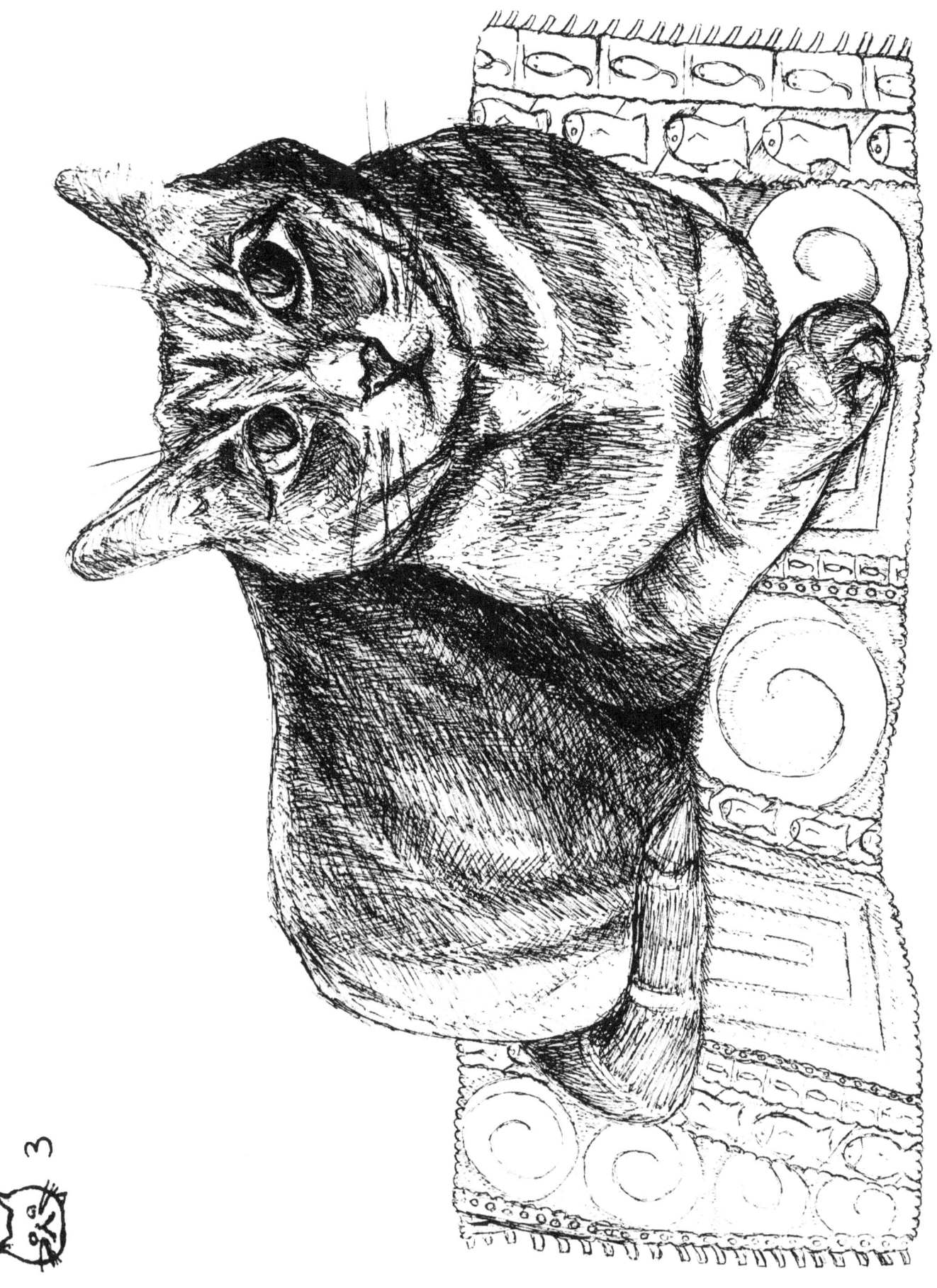

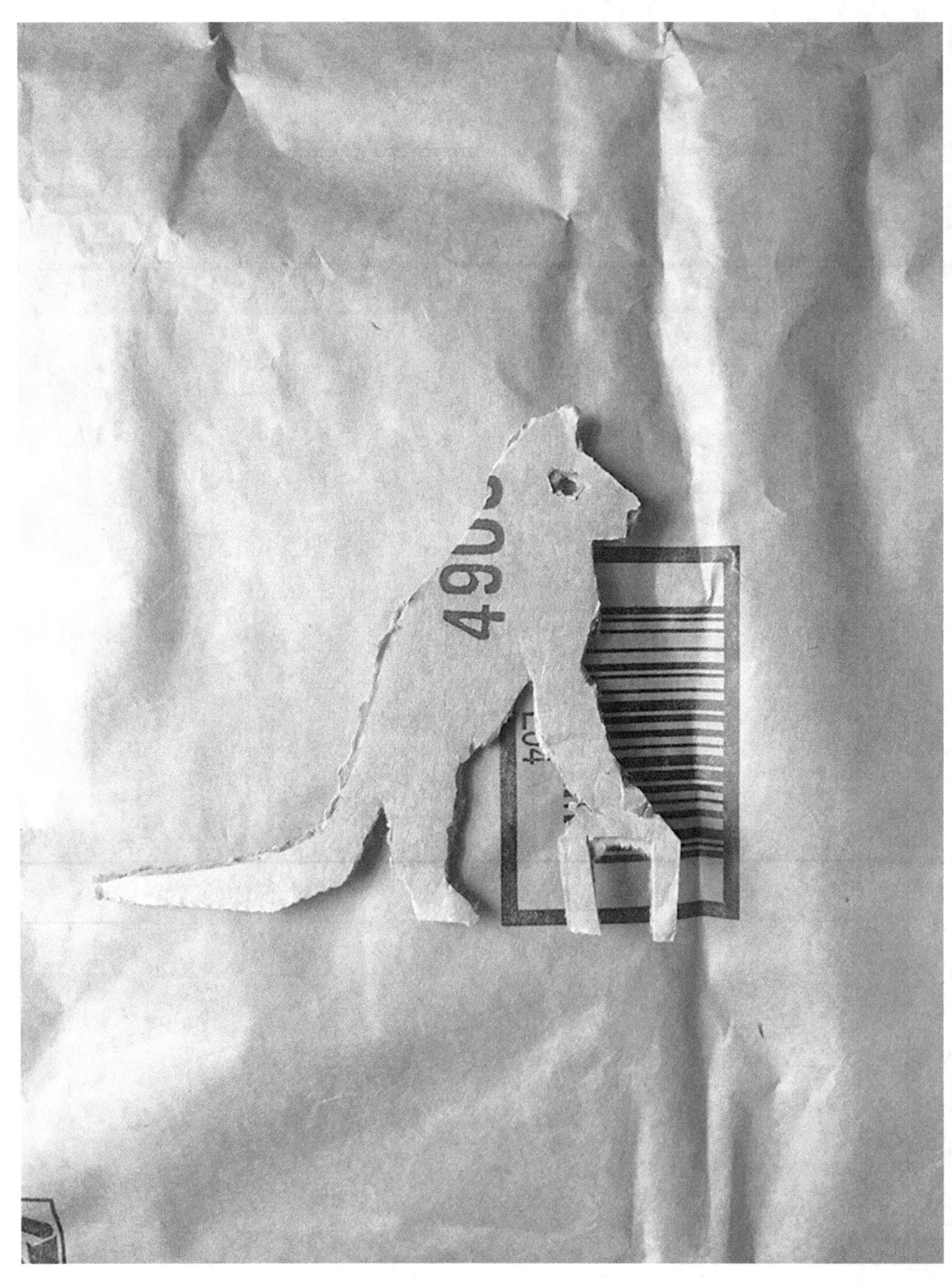

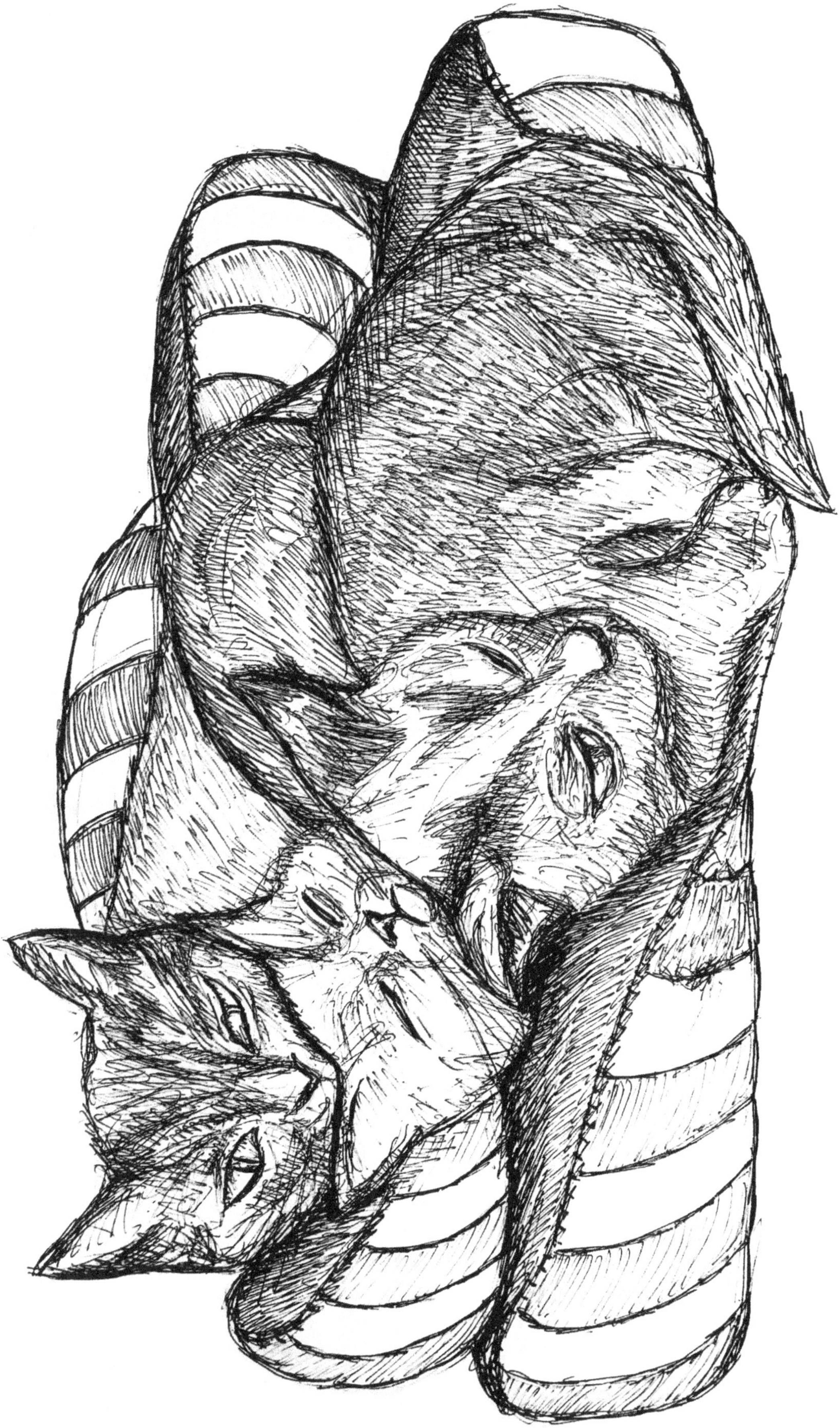

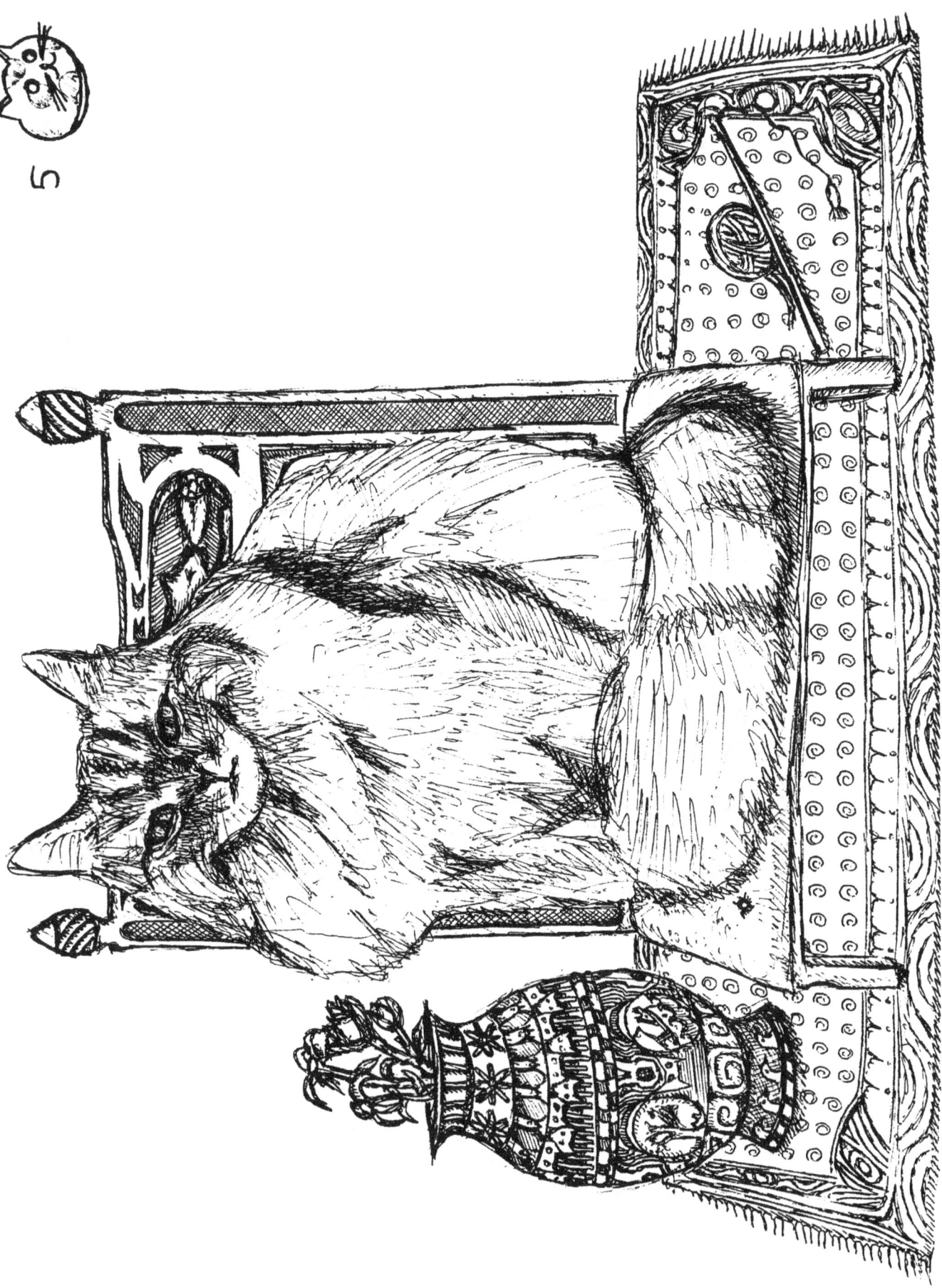

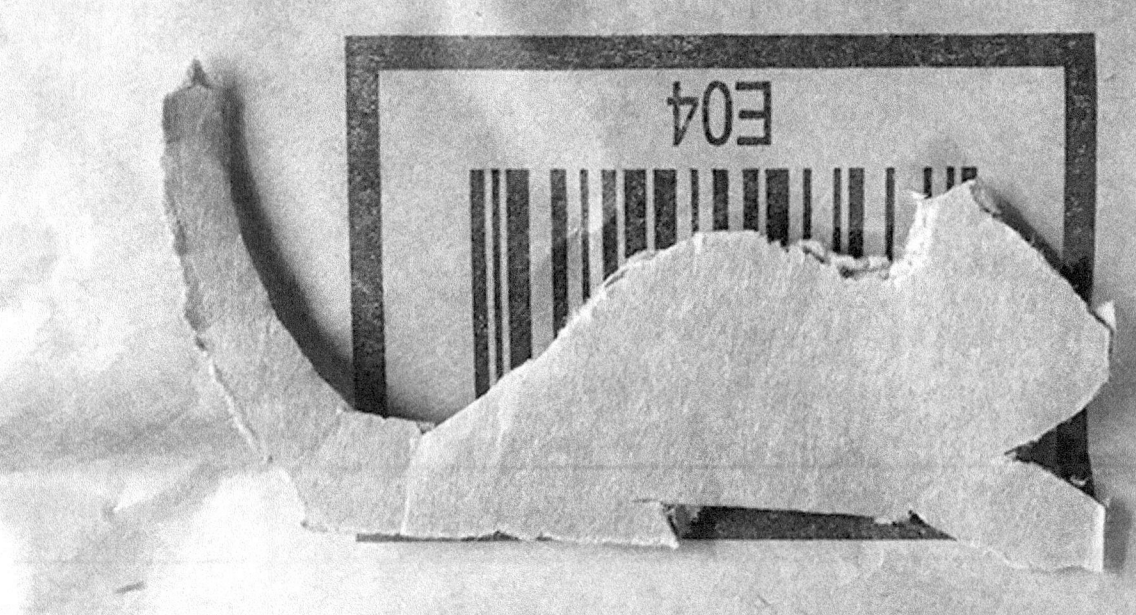

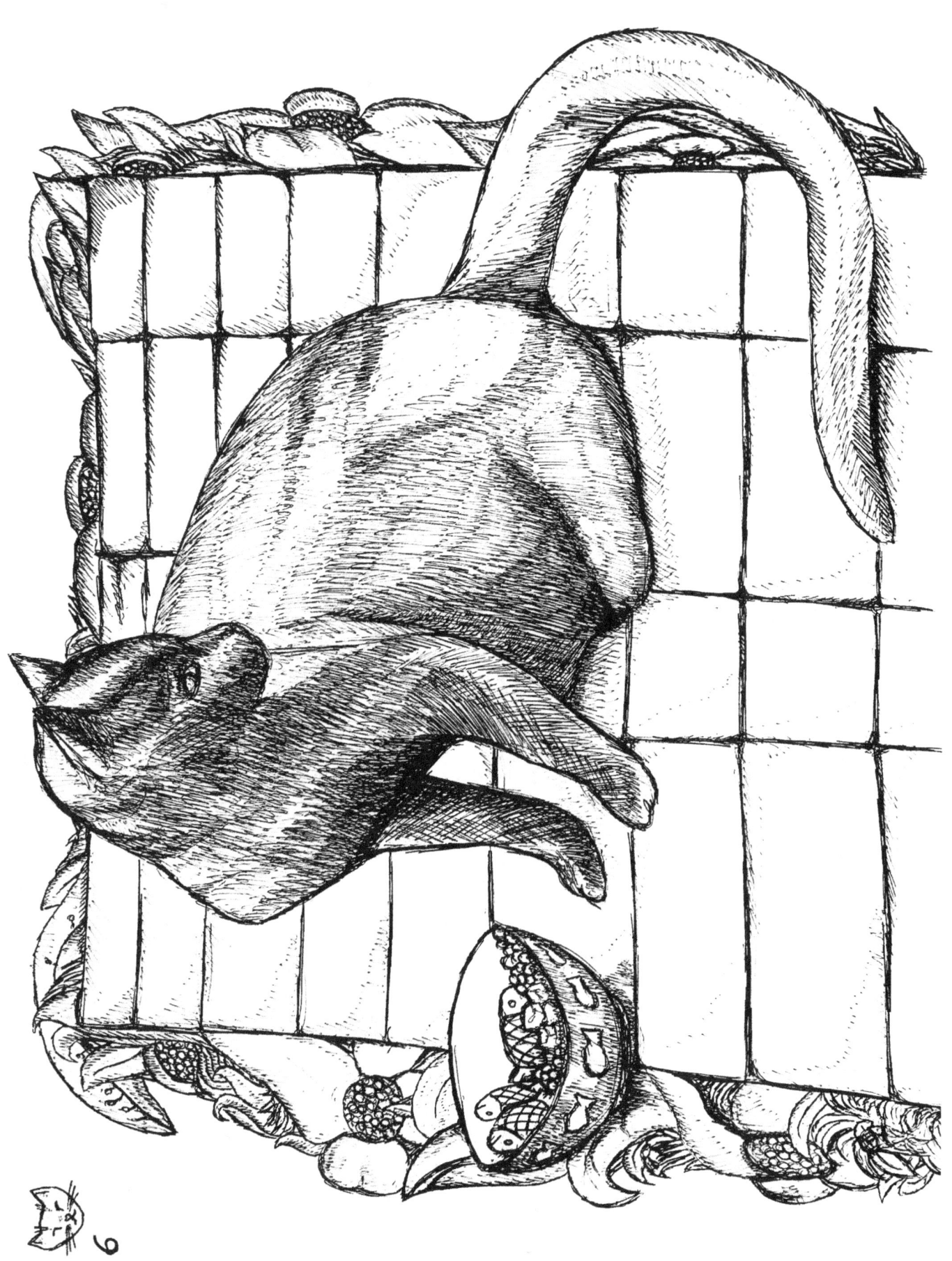

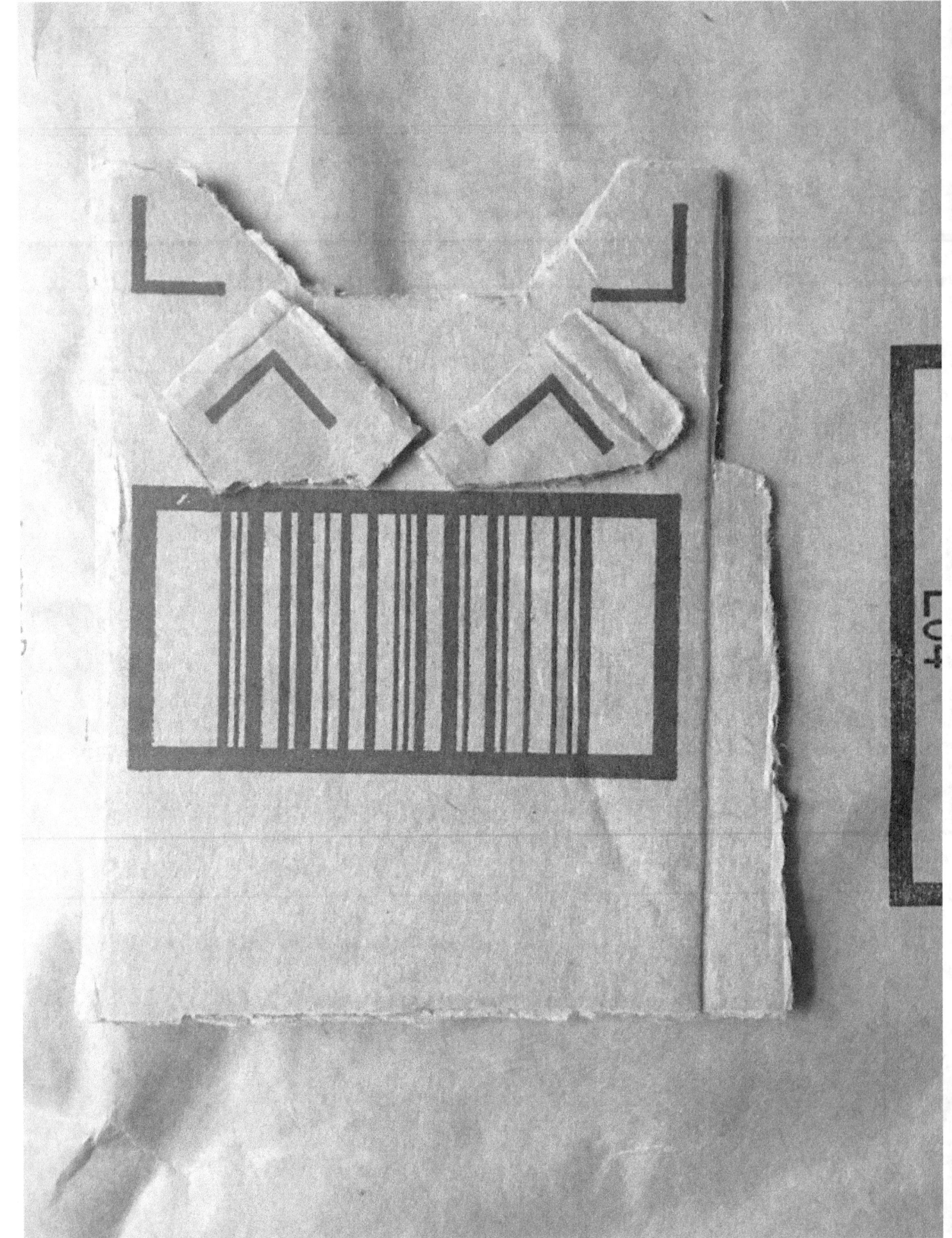

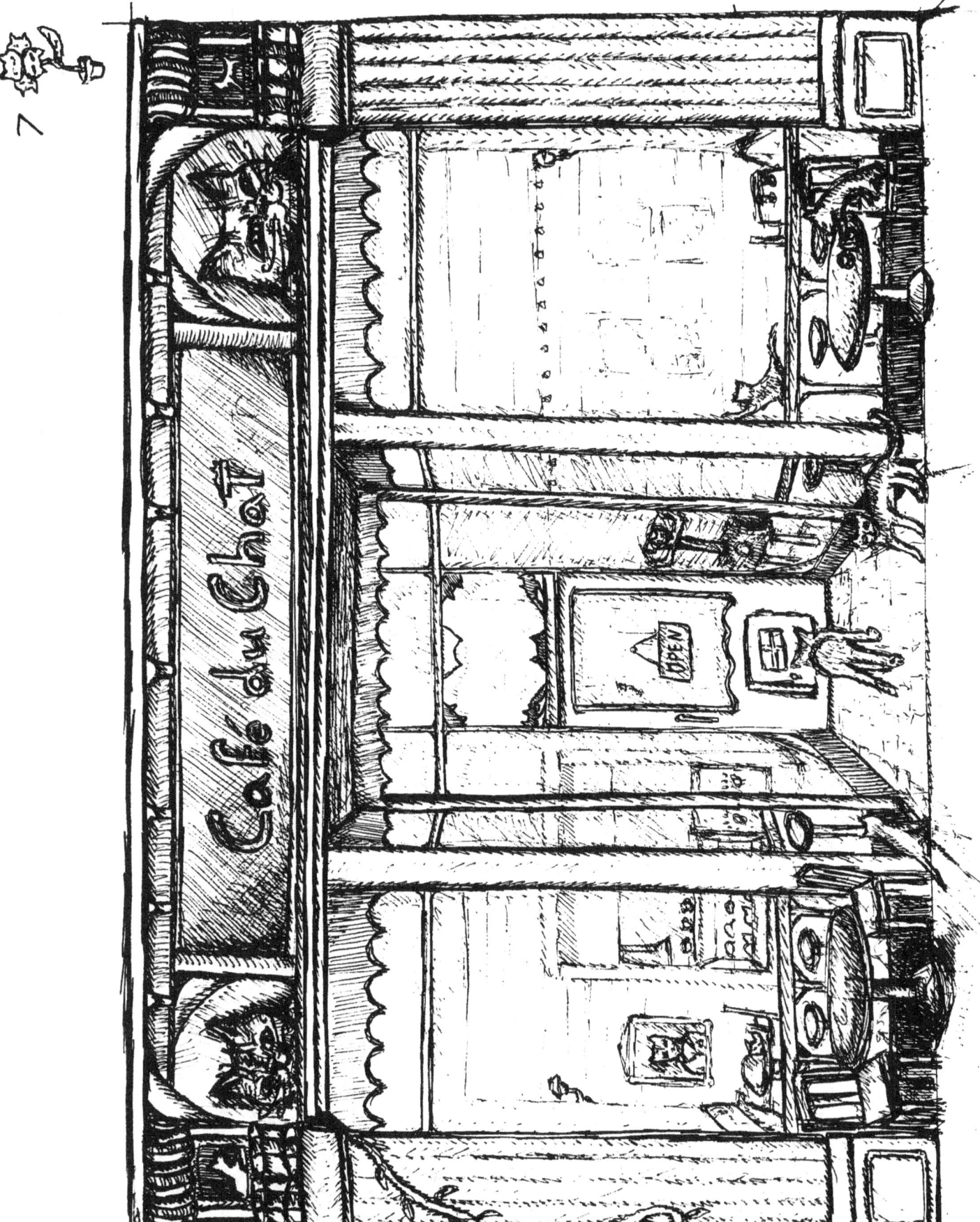

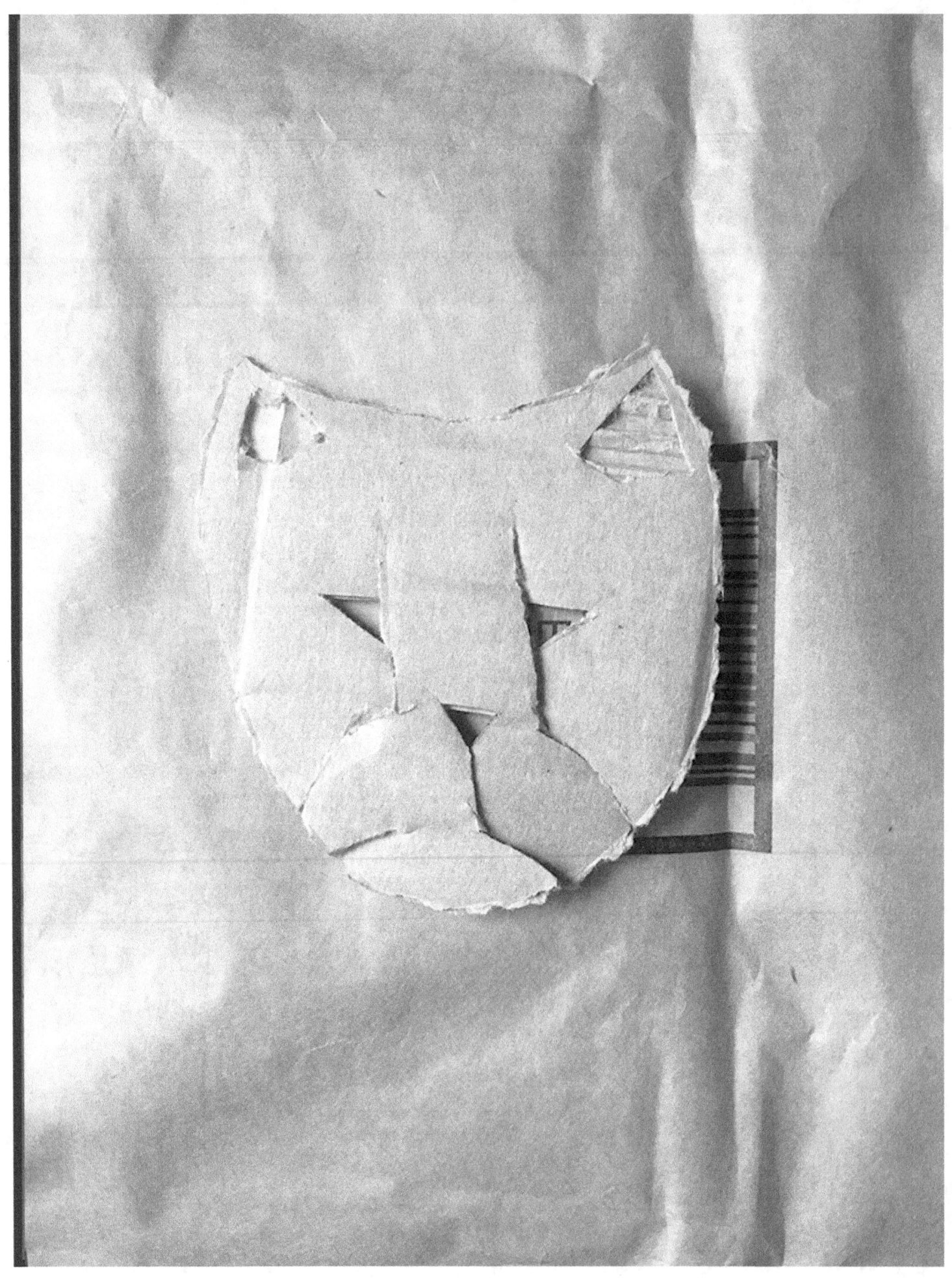

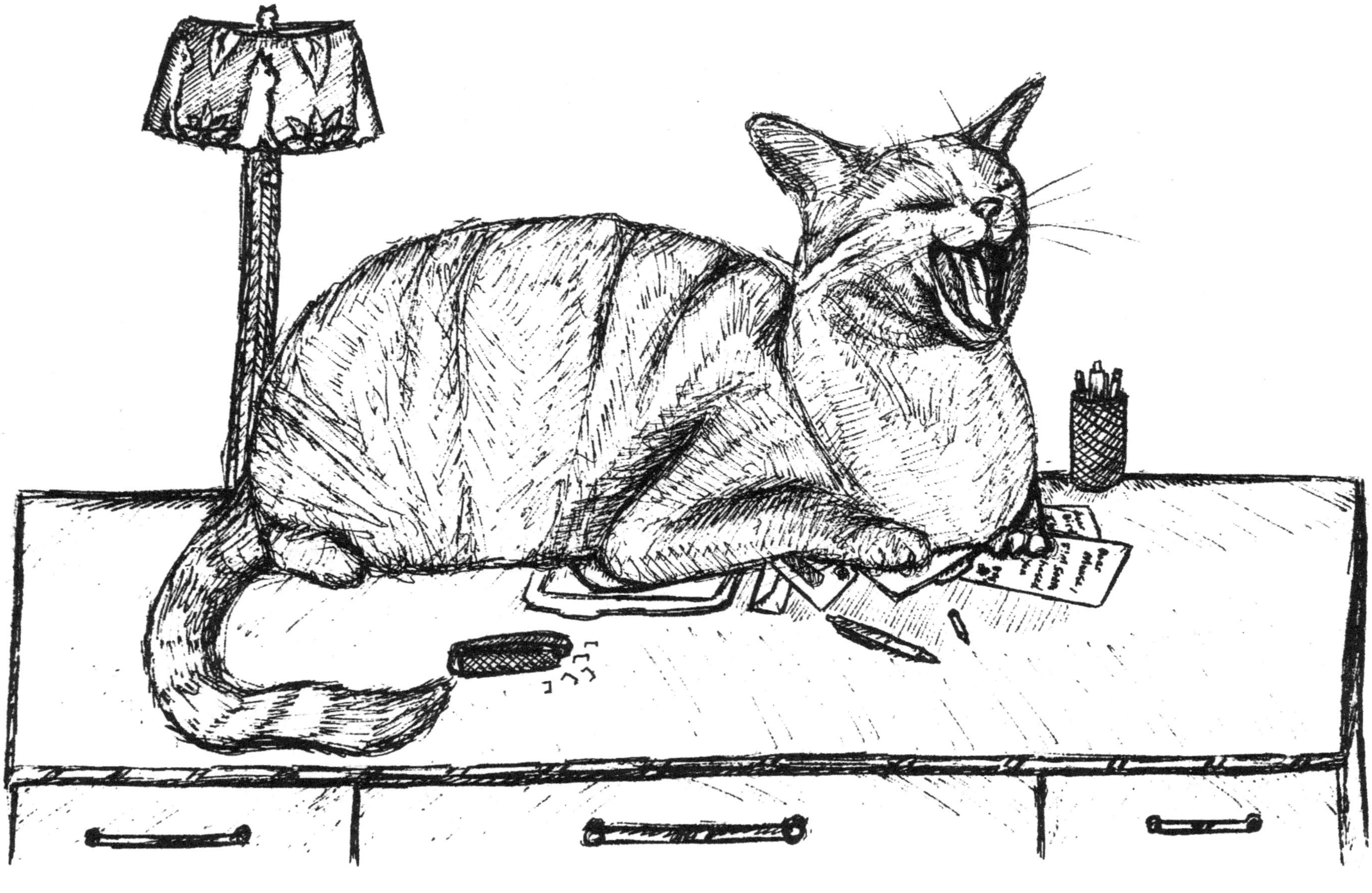

∞

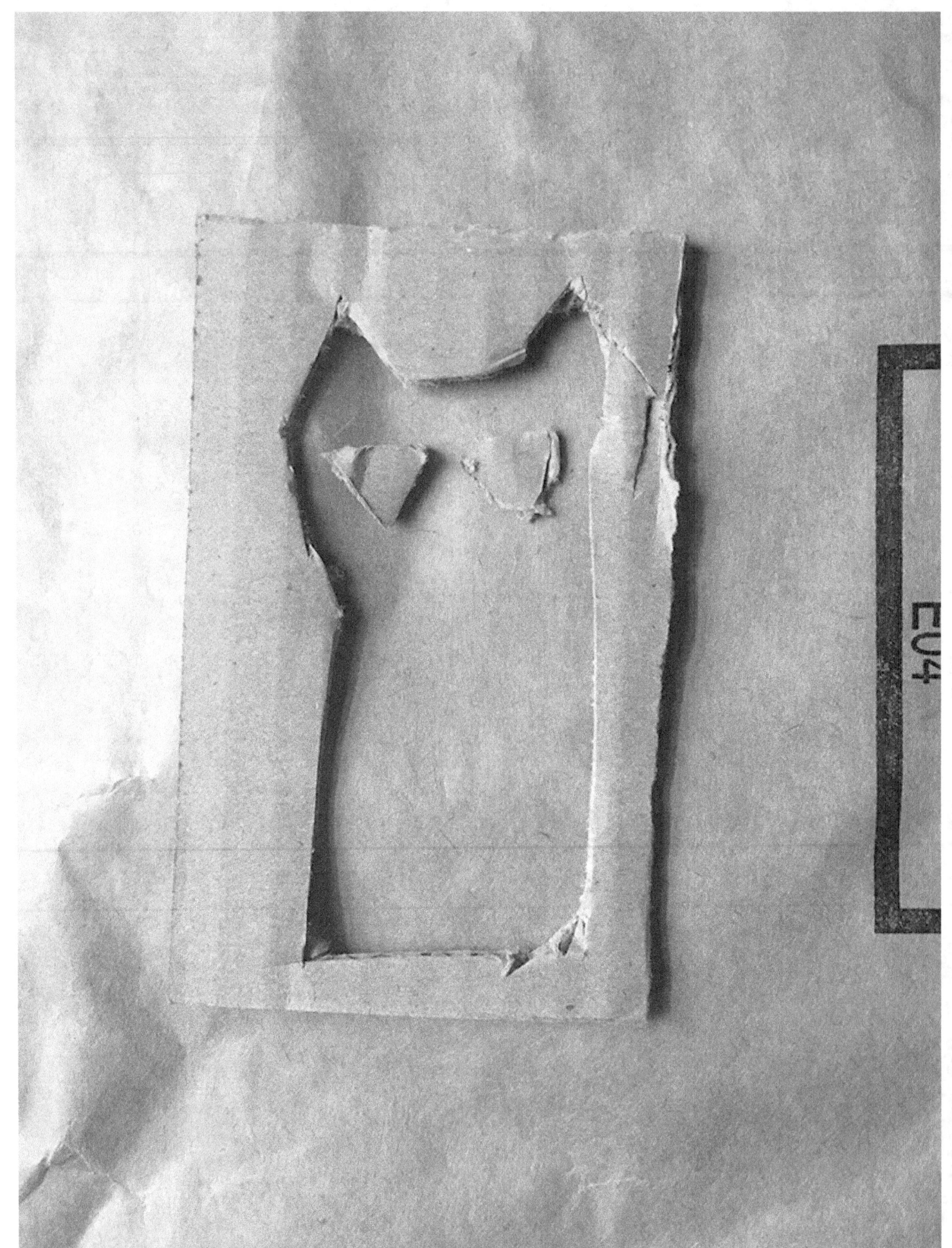

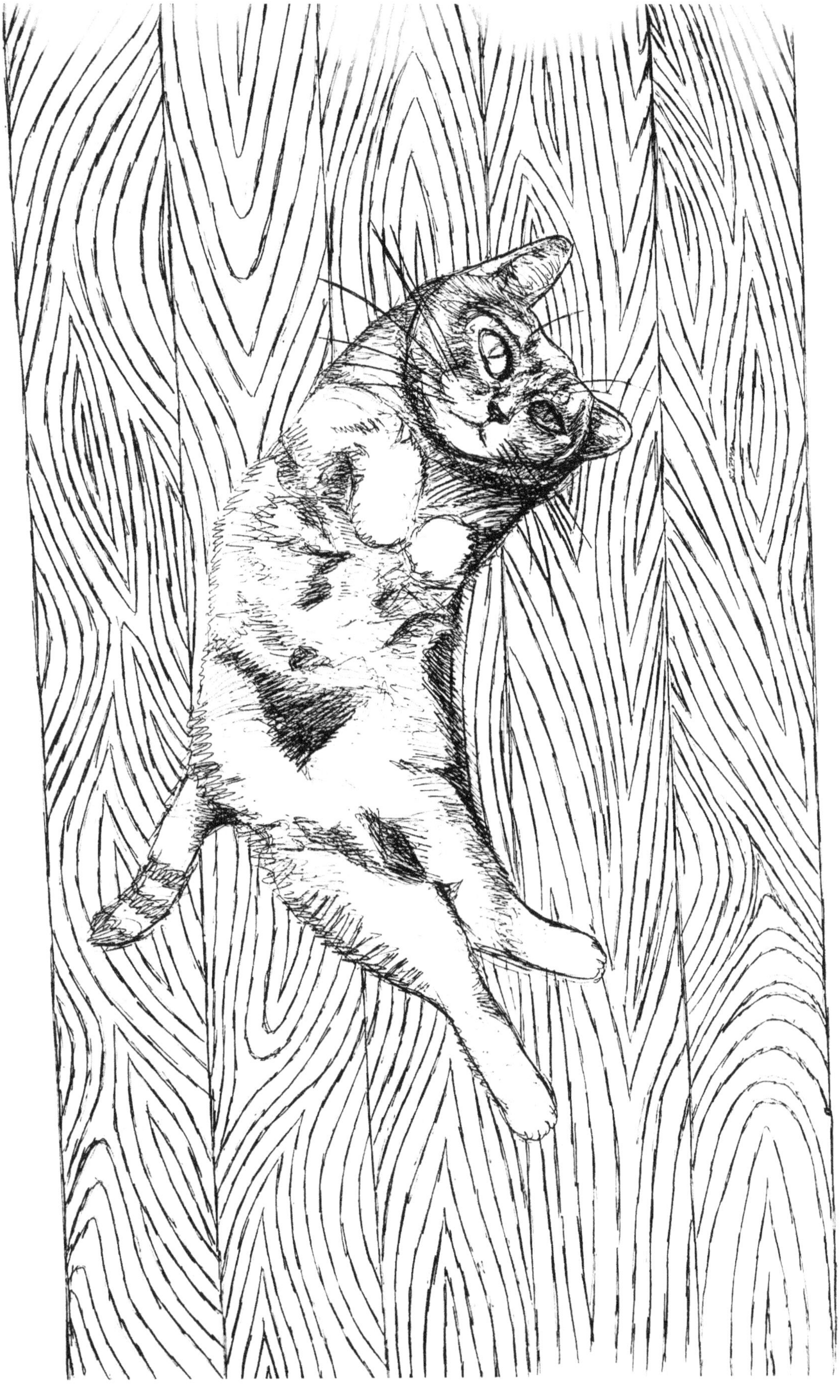

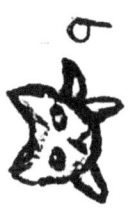

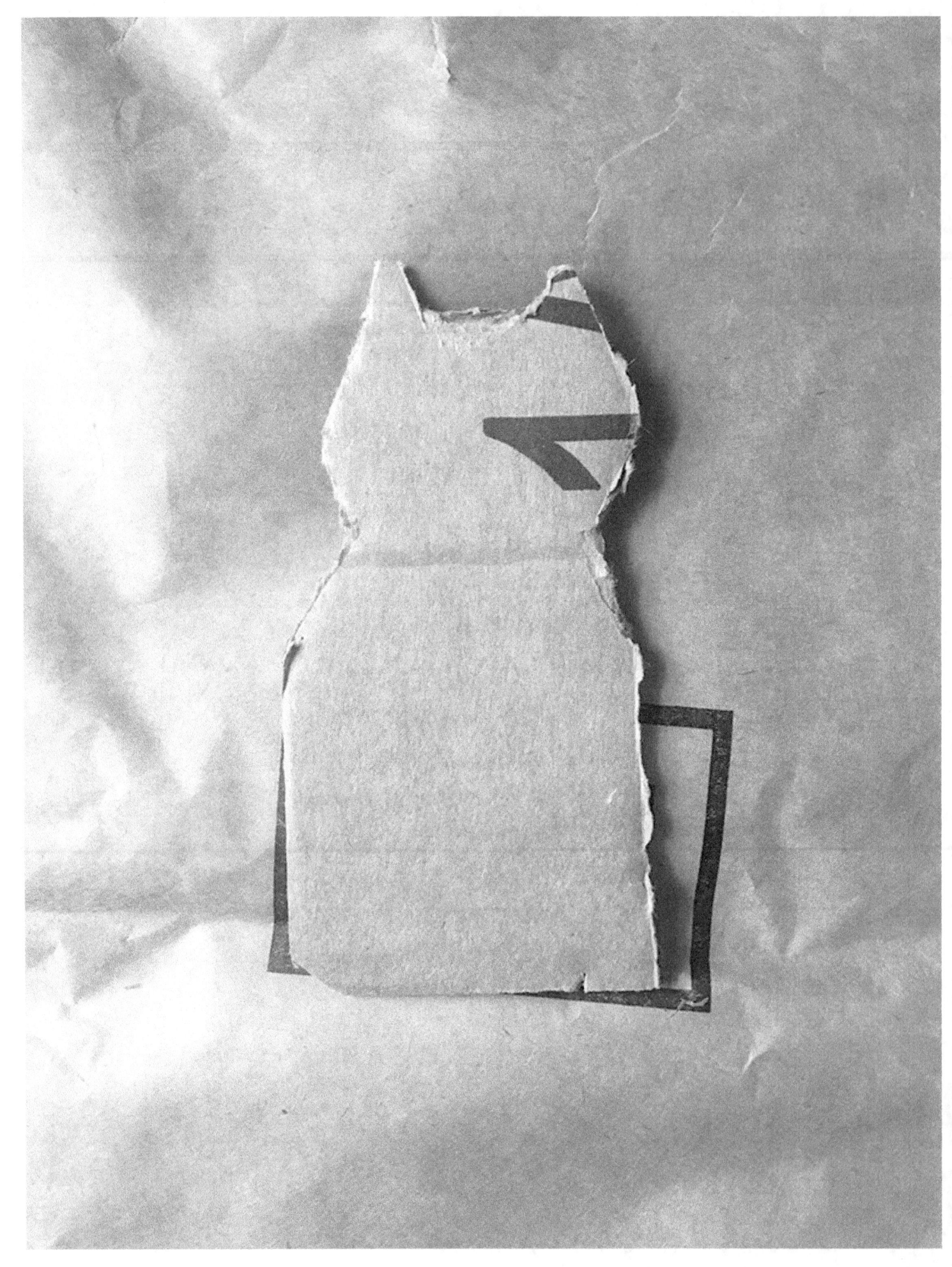

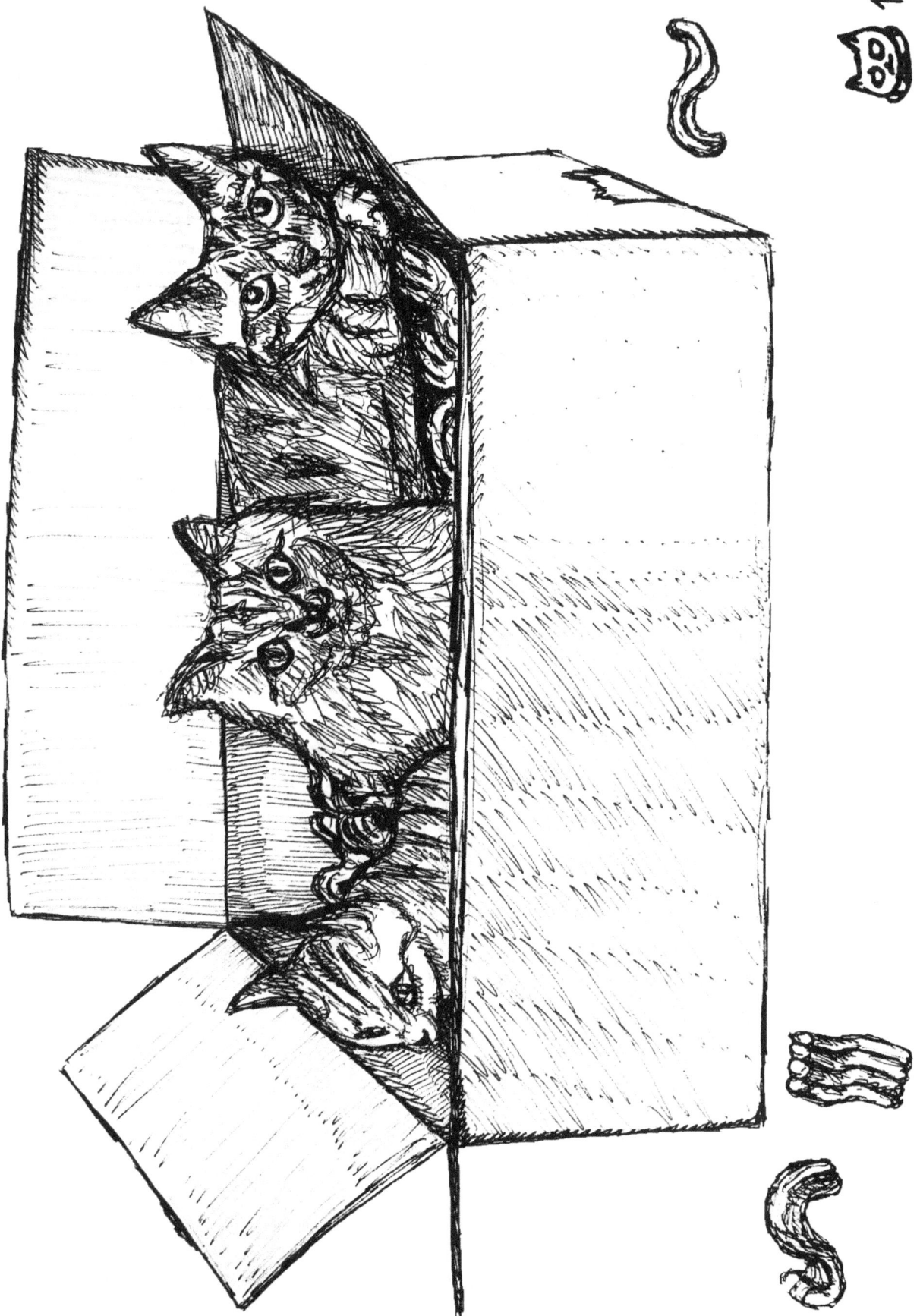

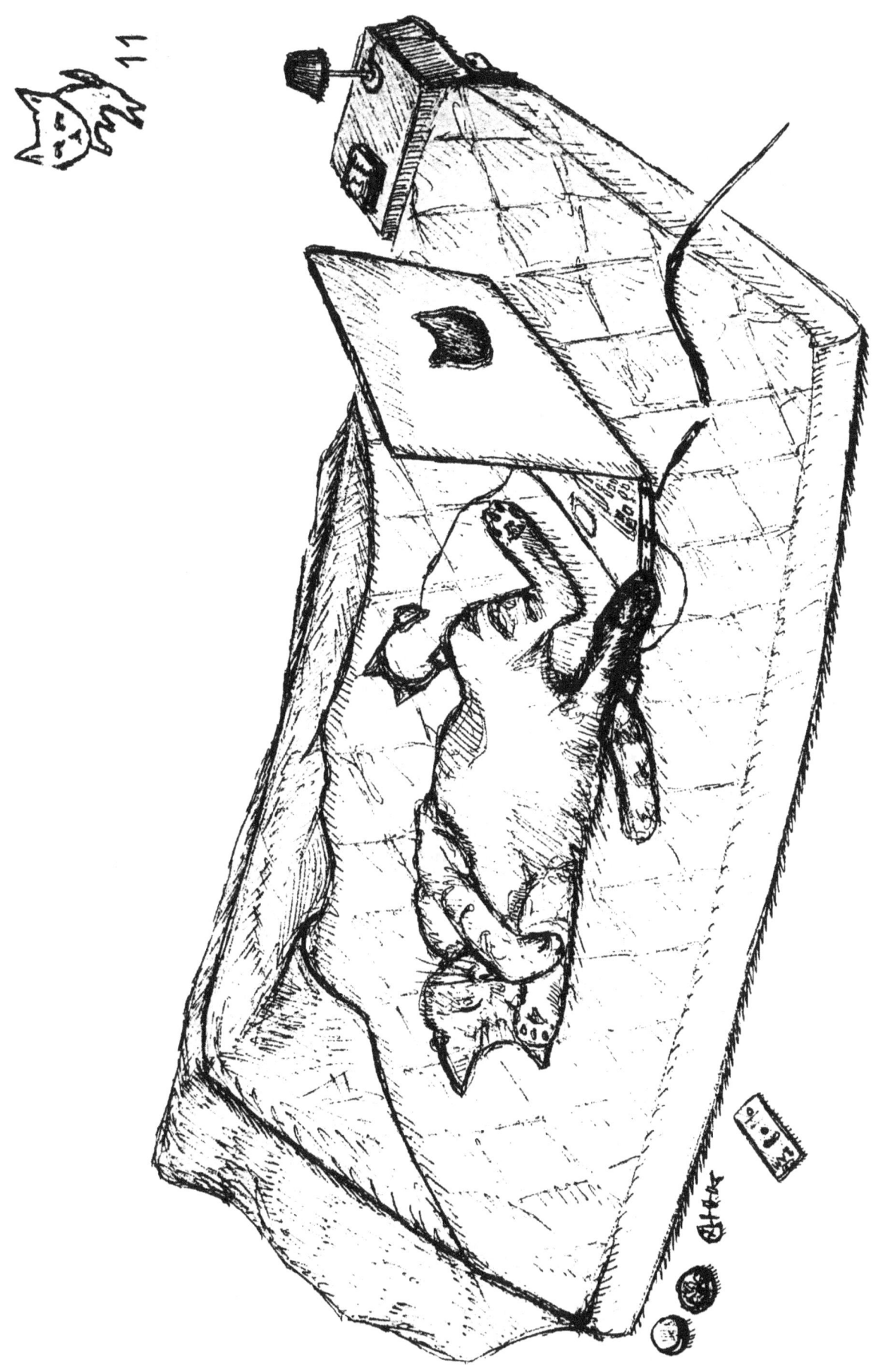

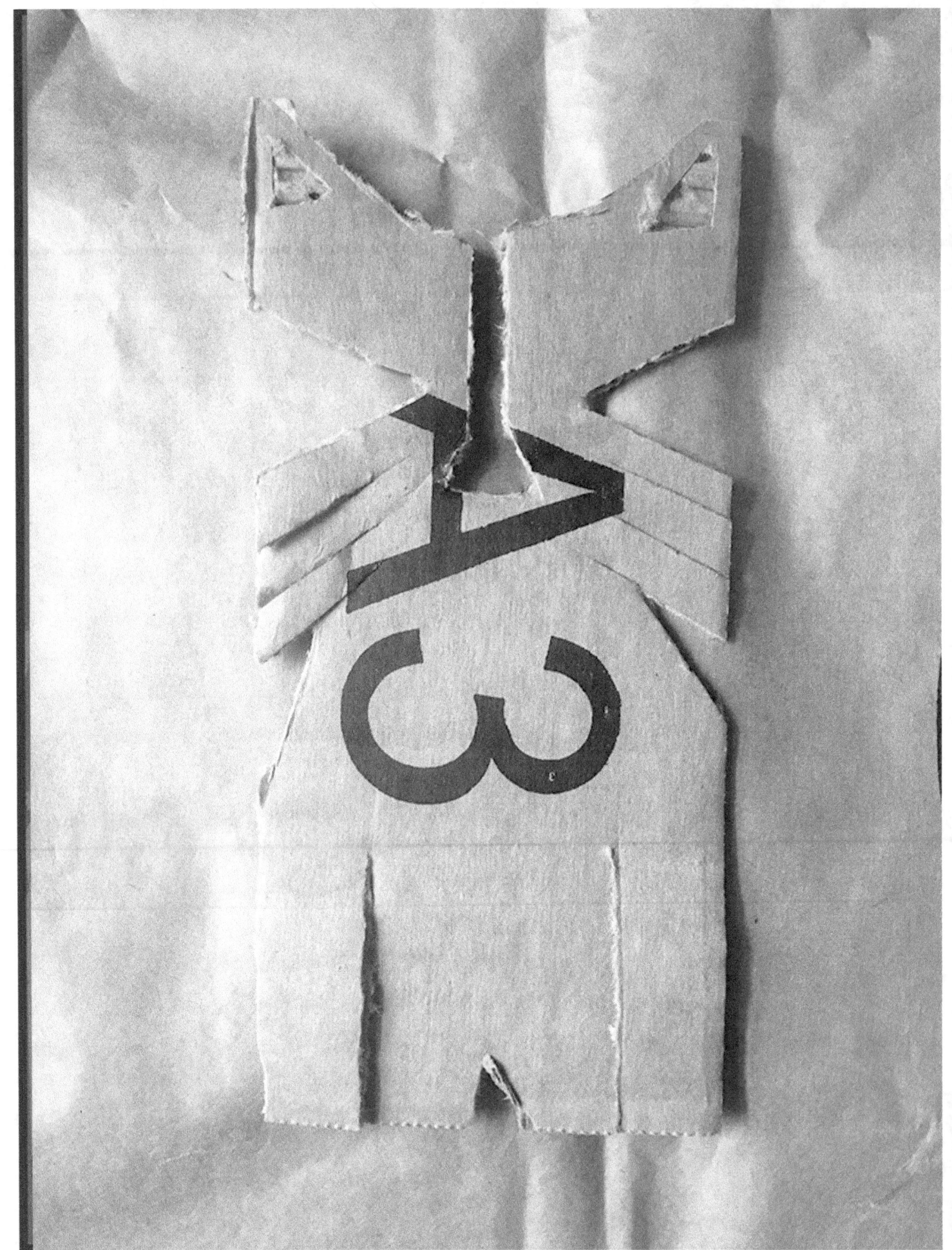

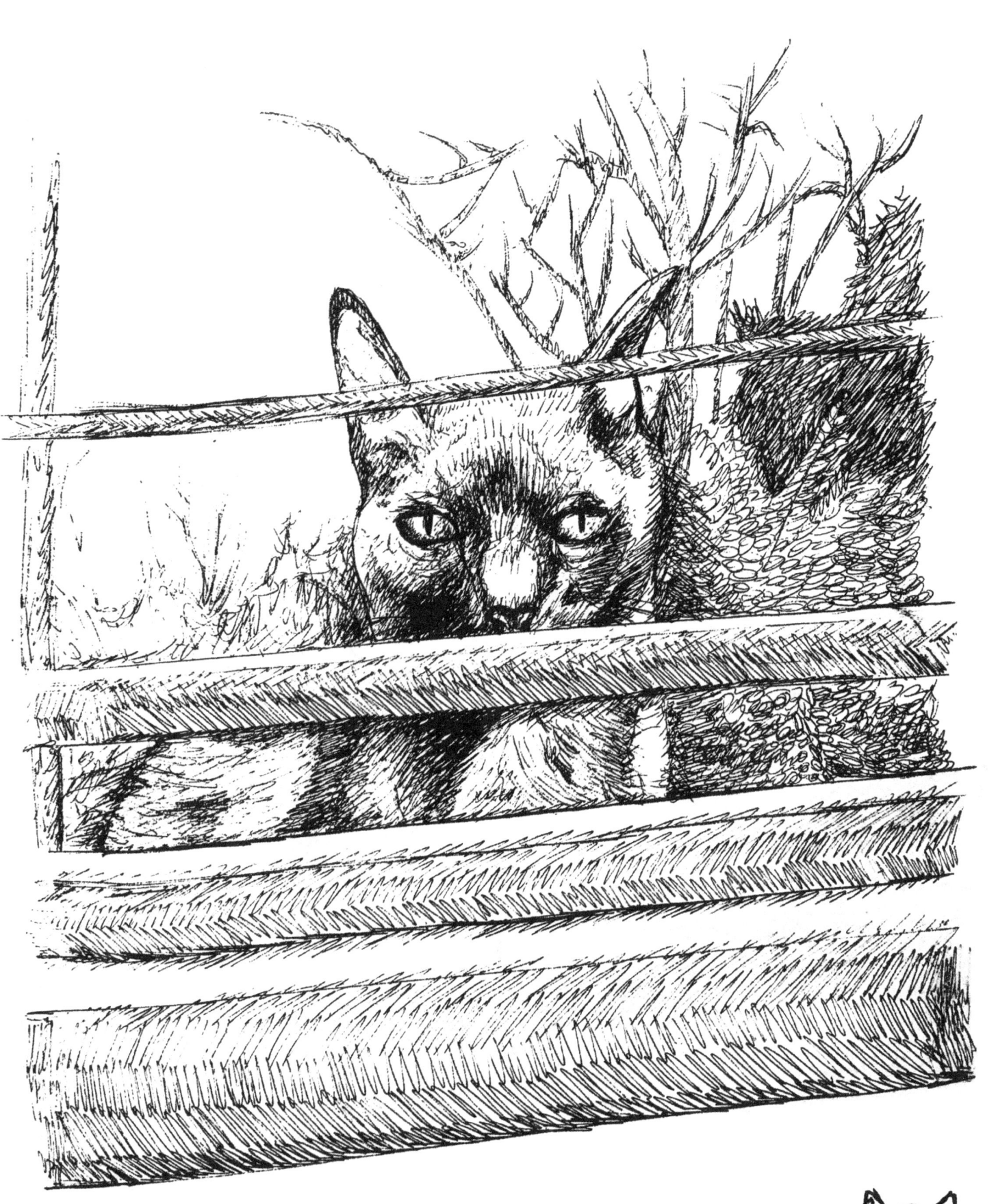

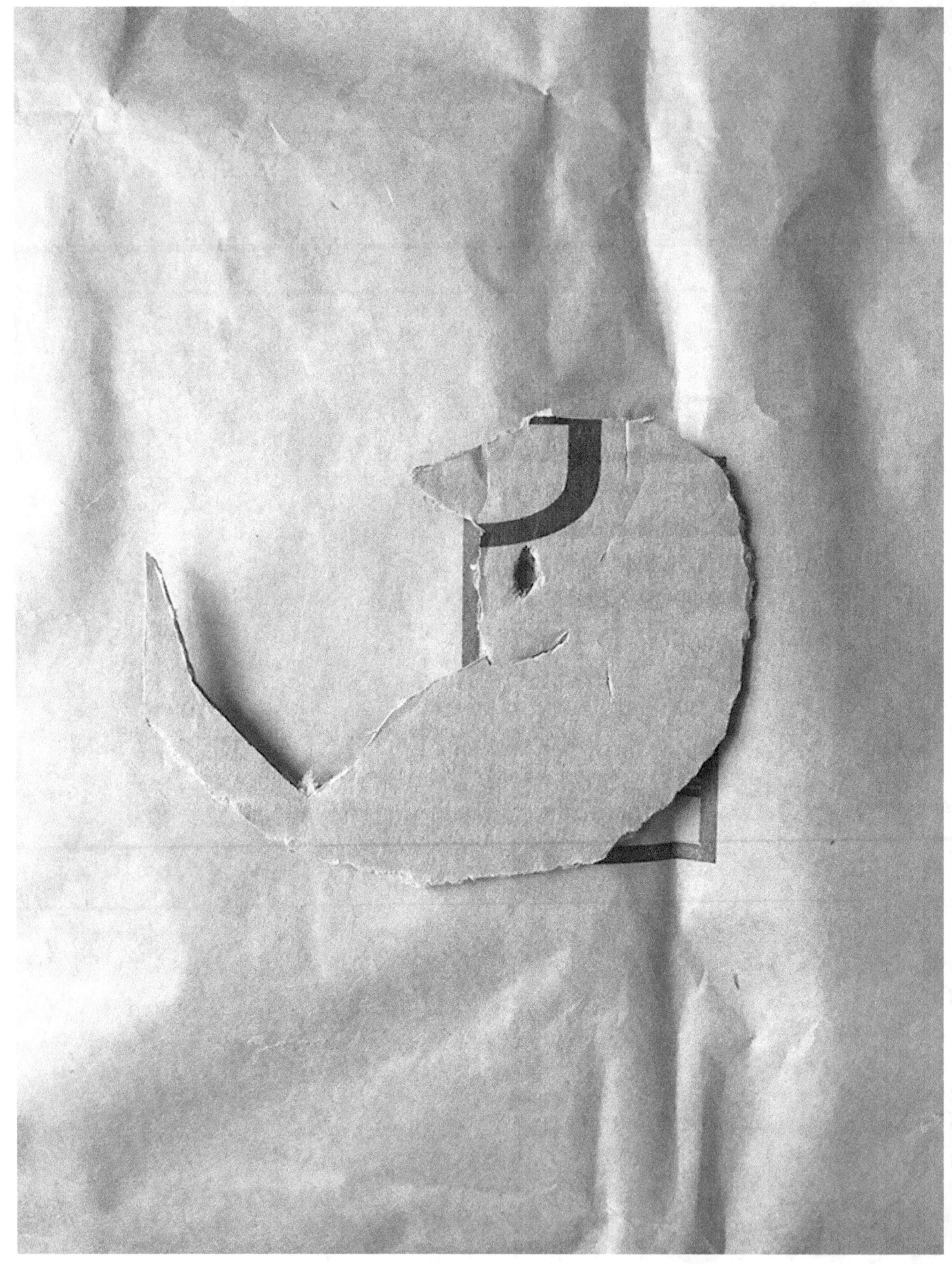

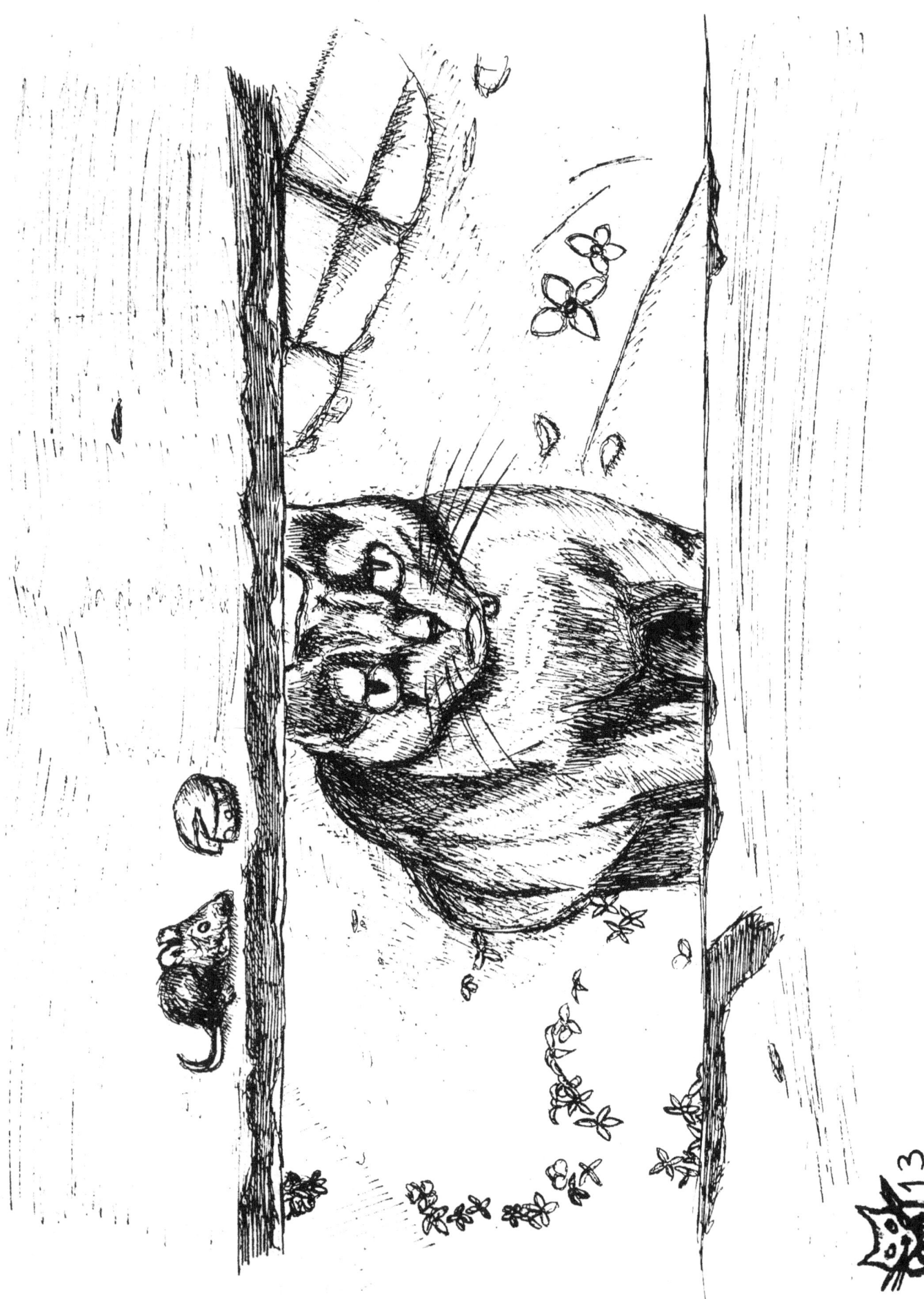

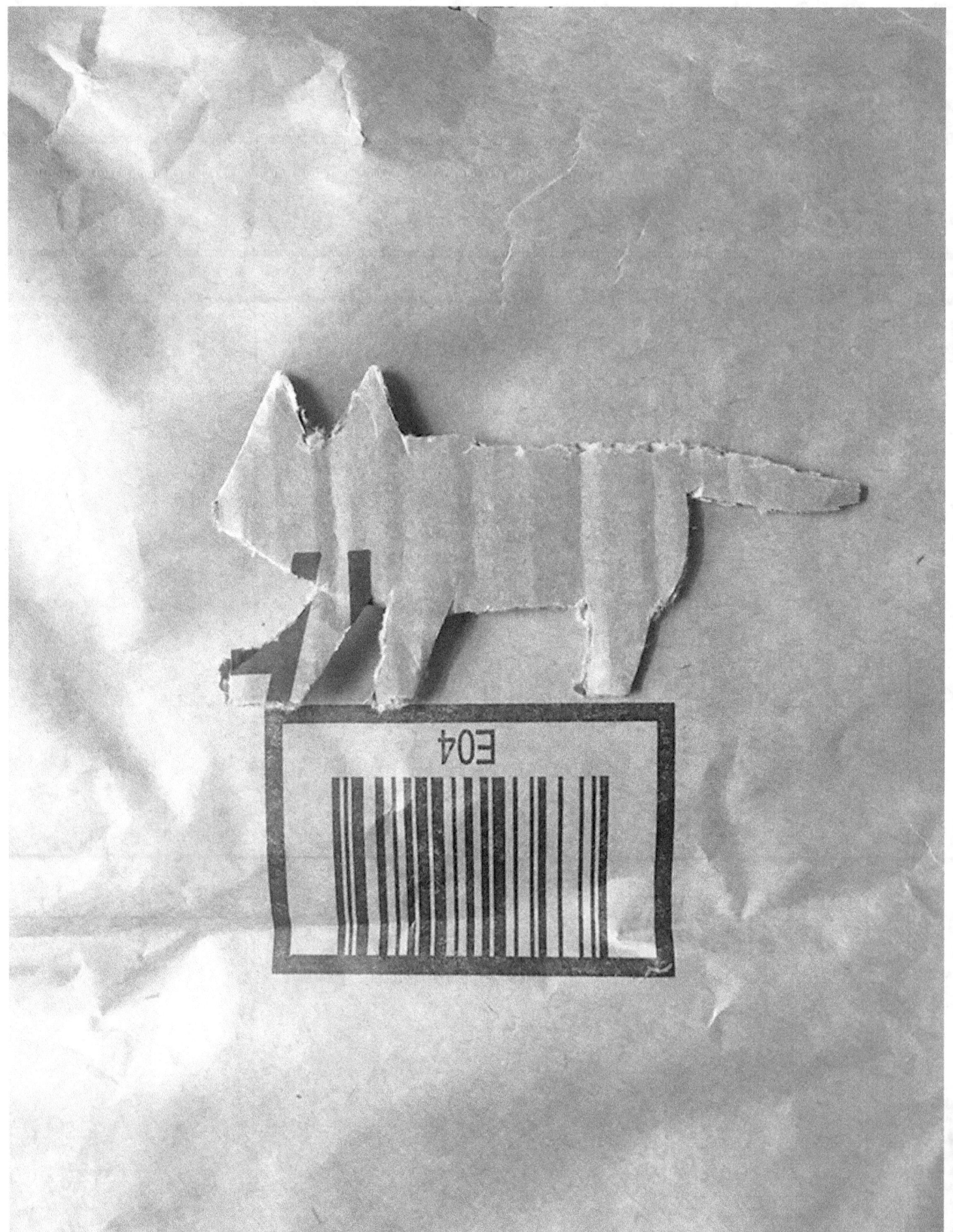

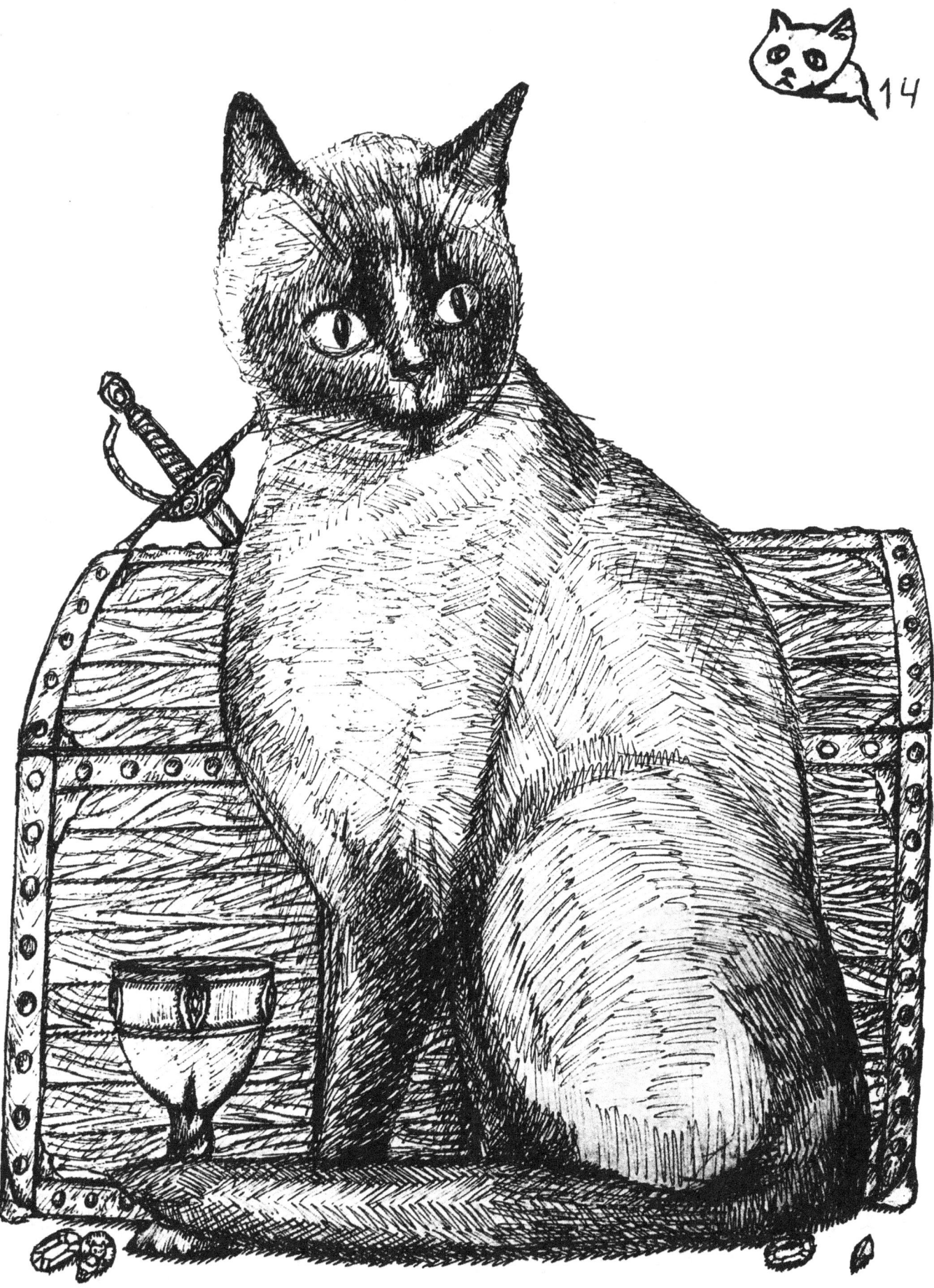

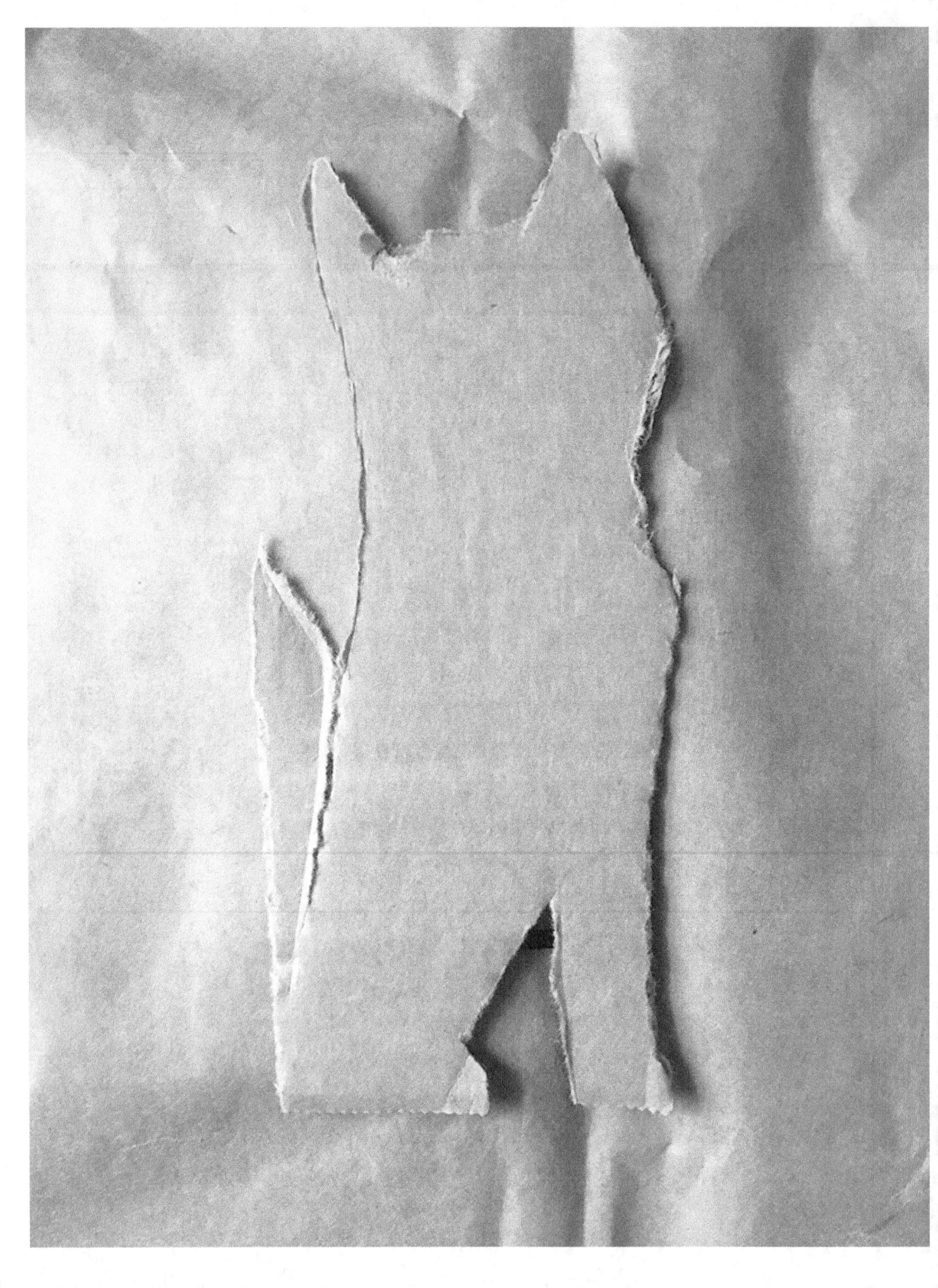

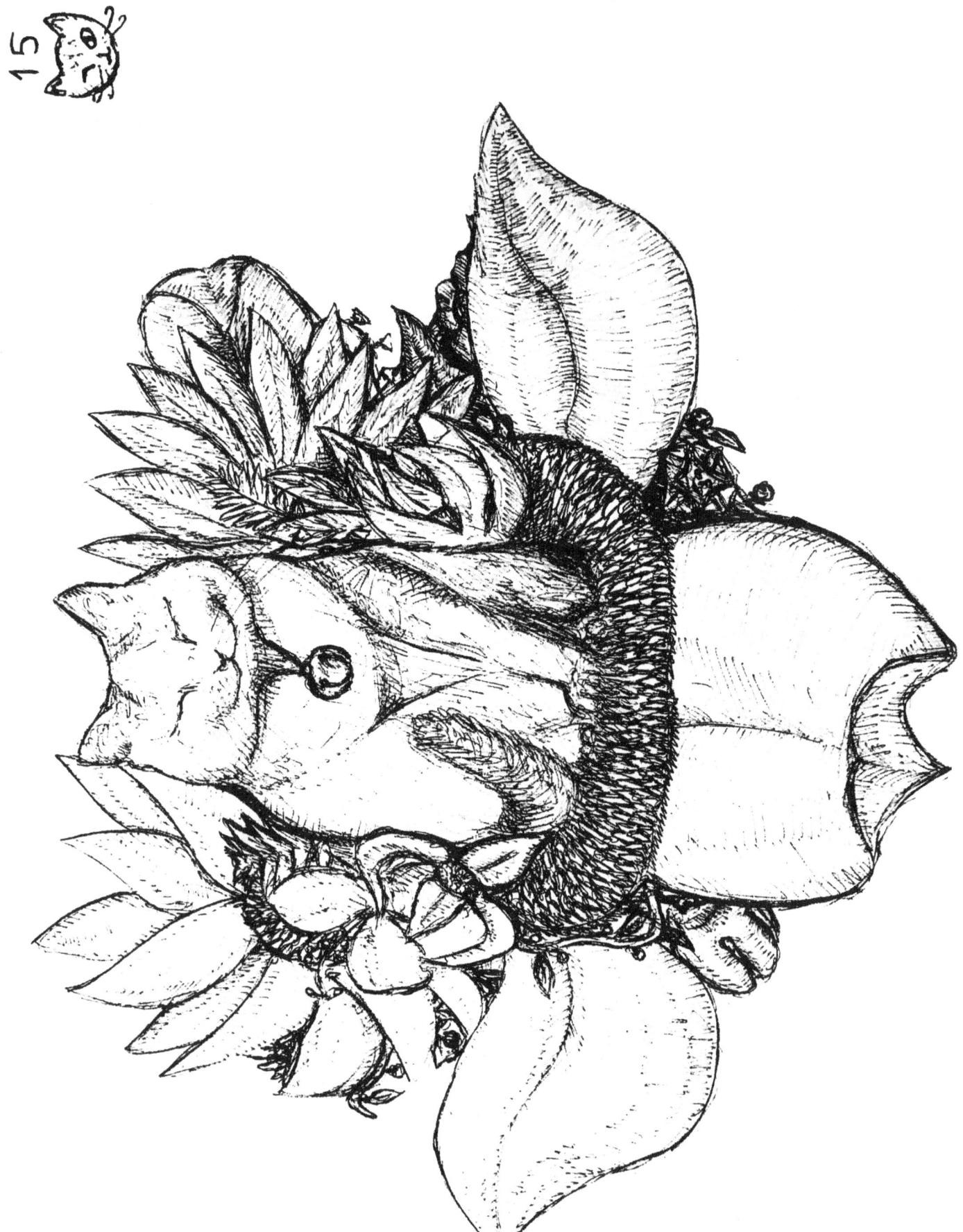

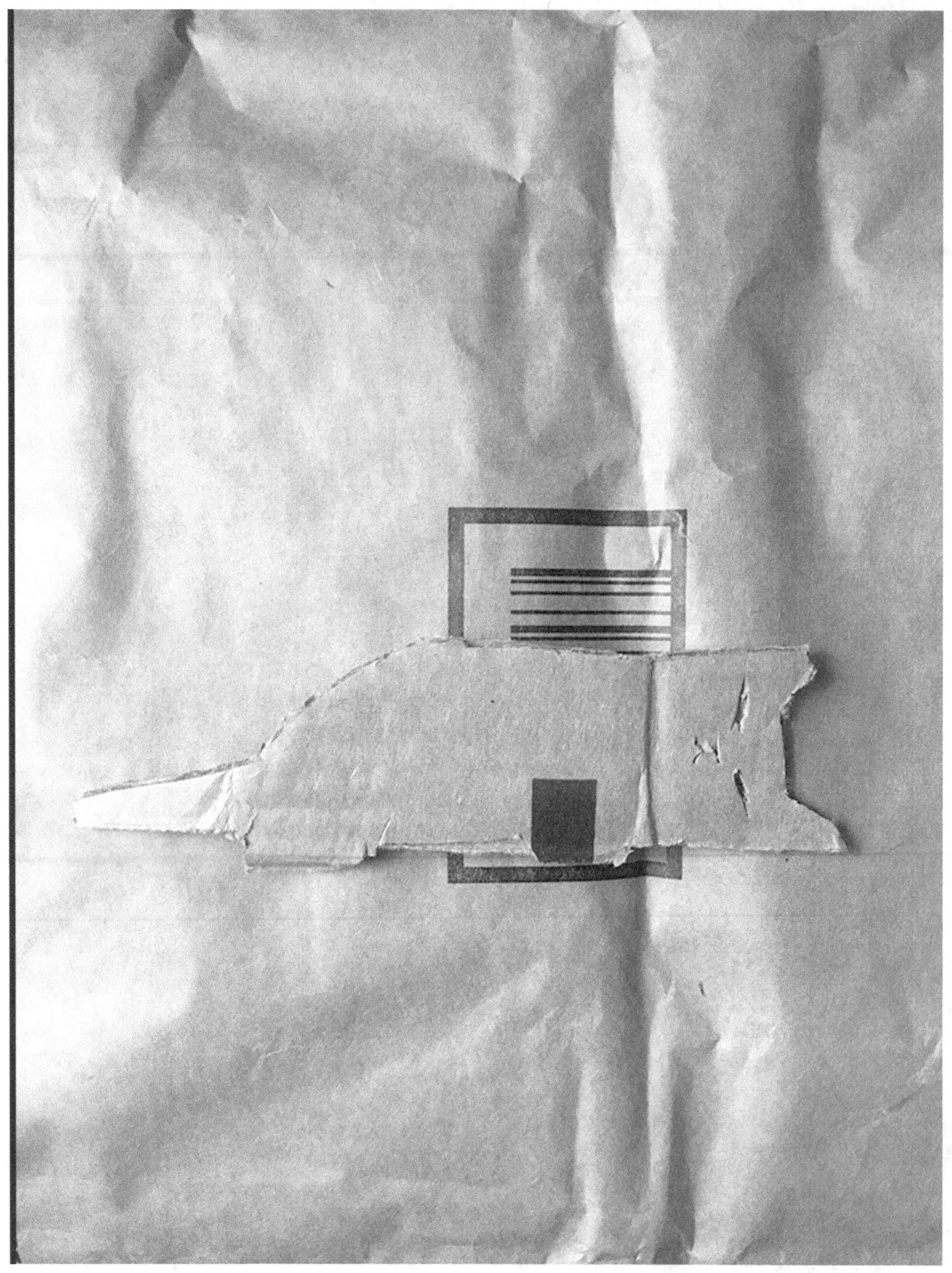

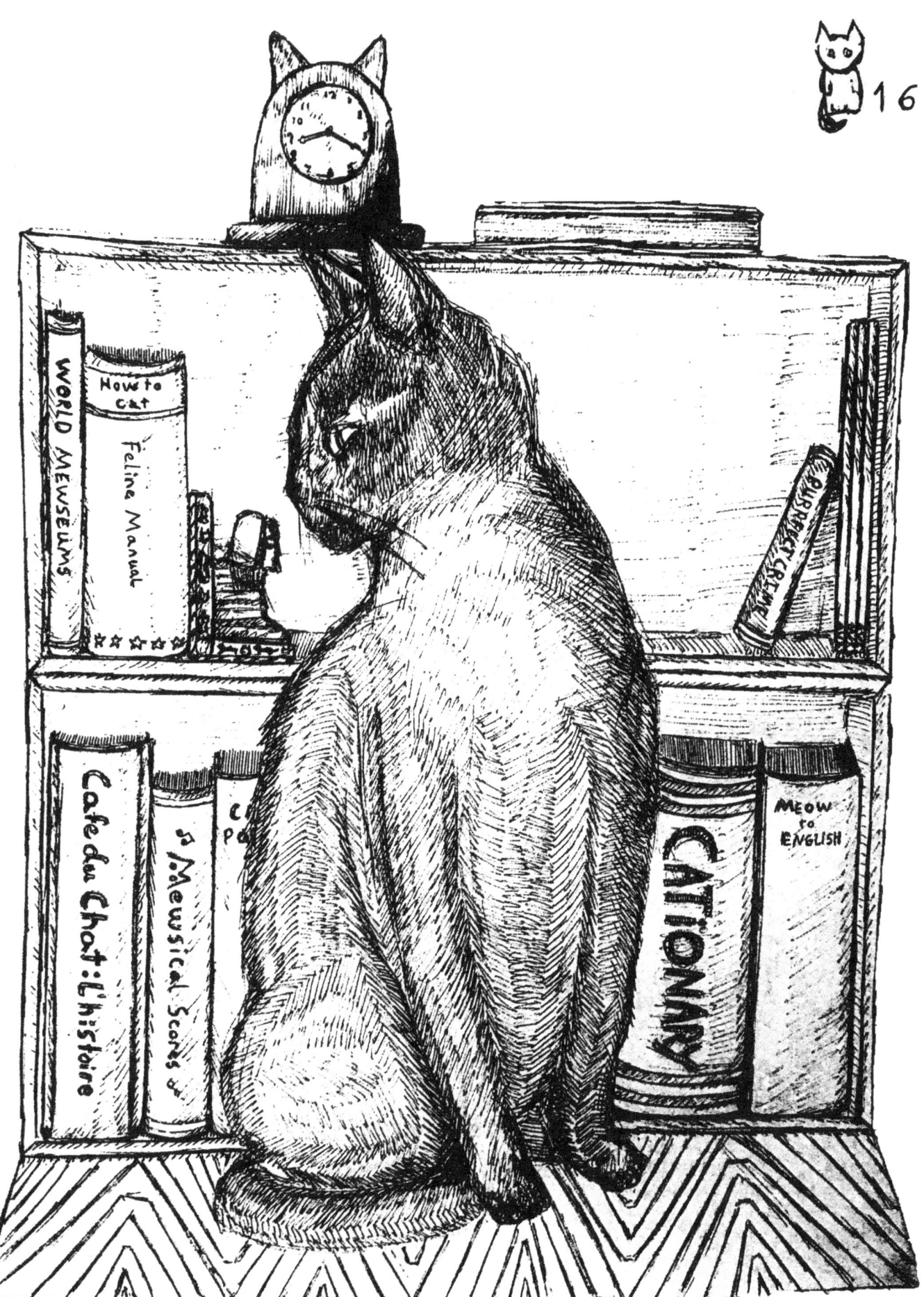

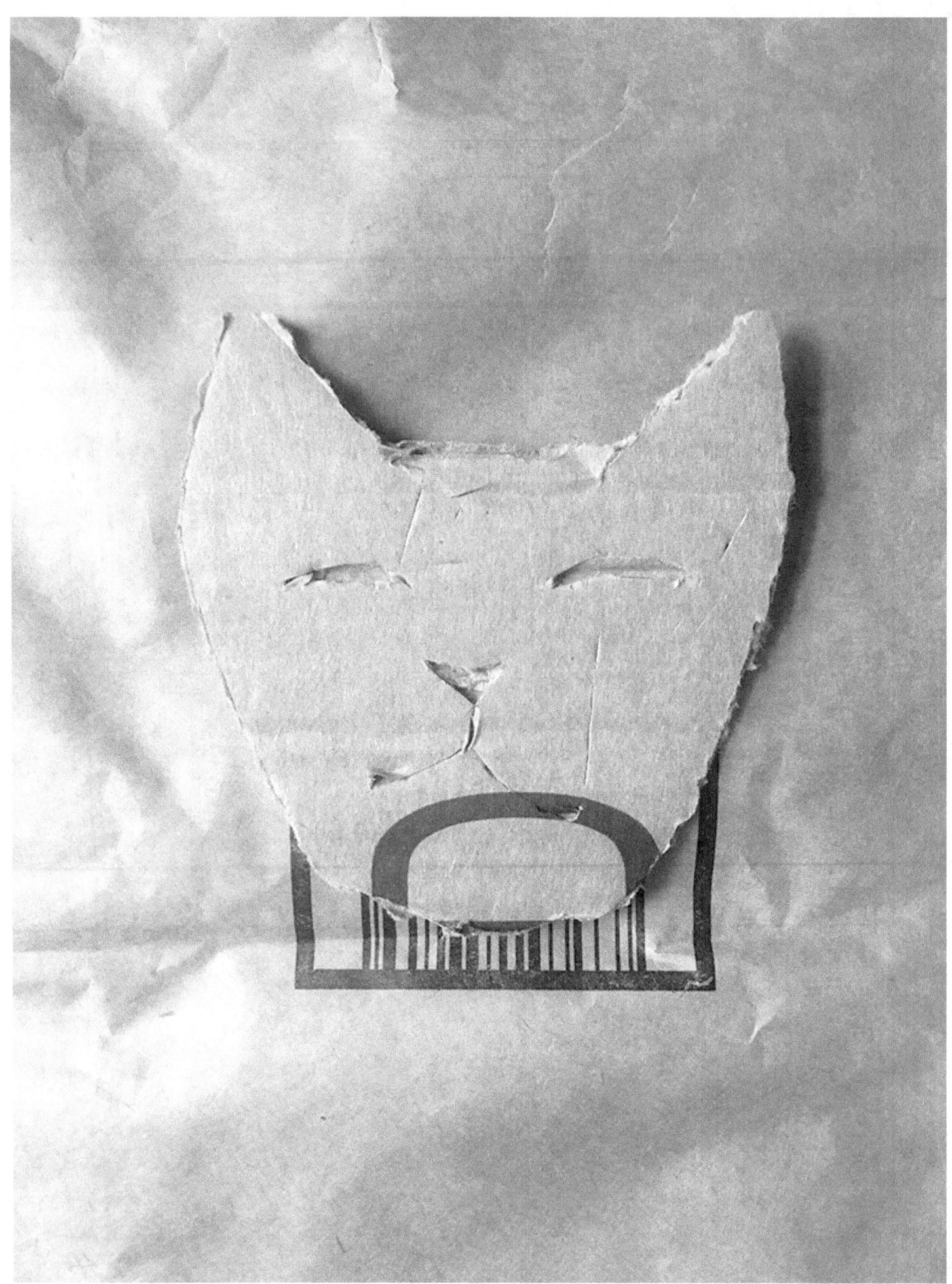

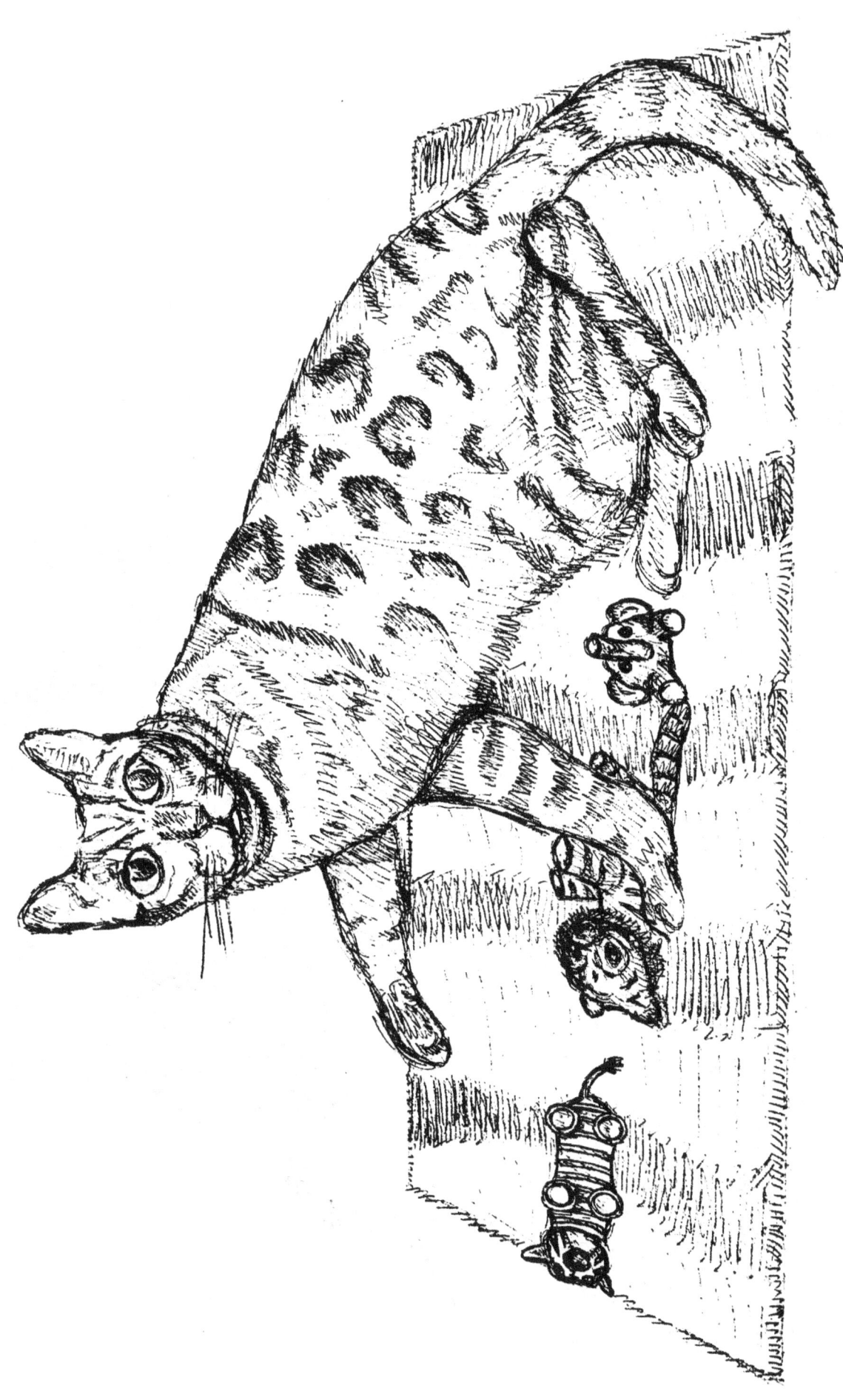

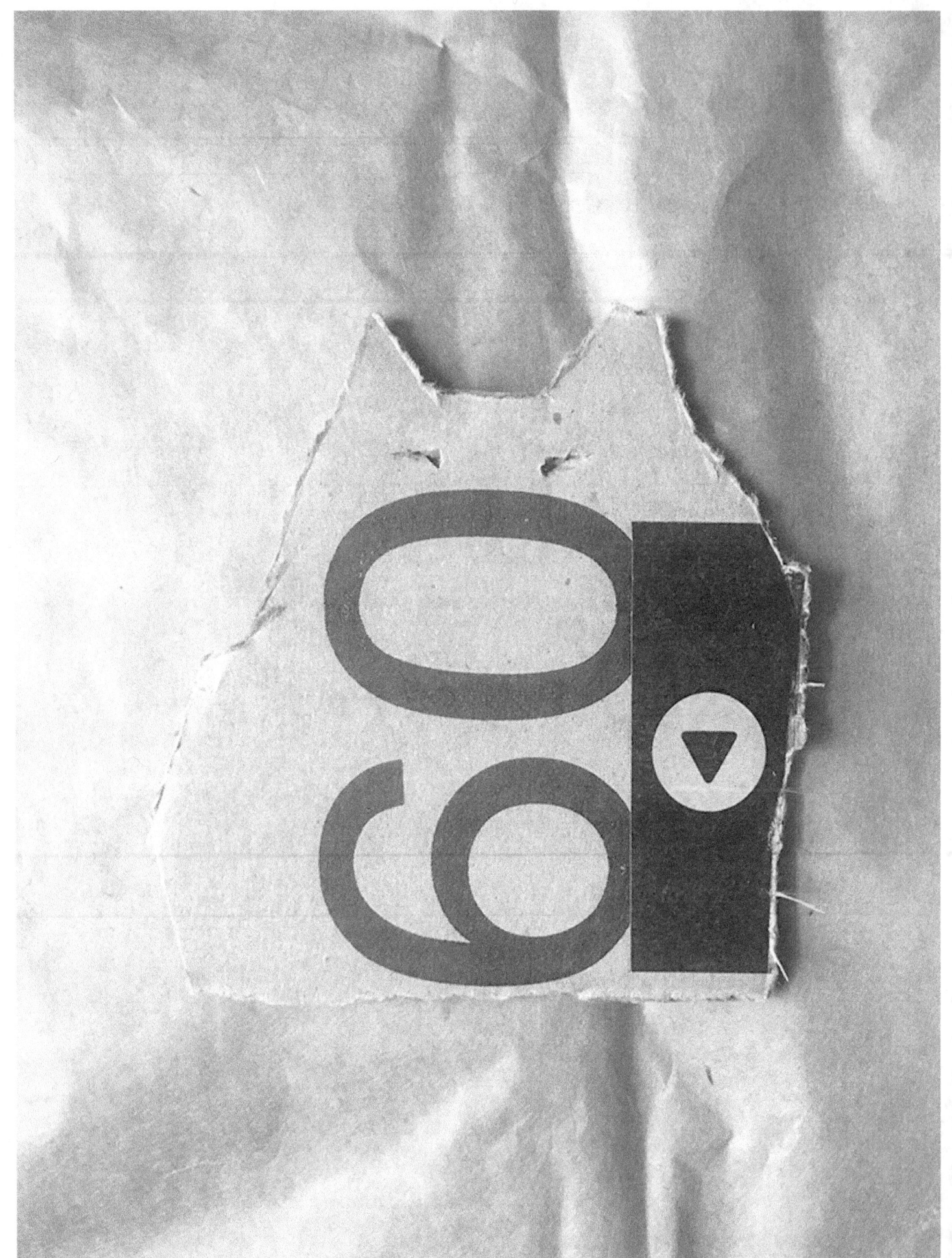

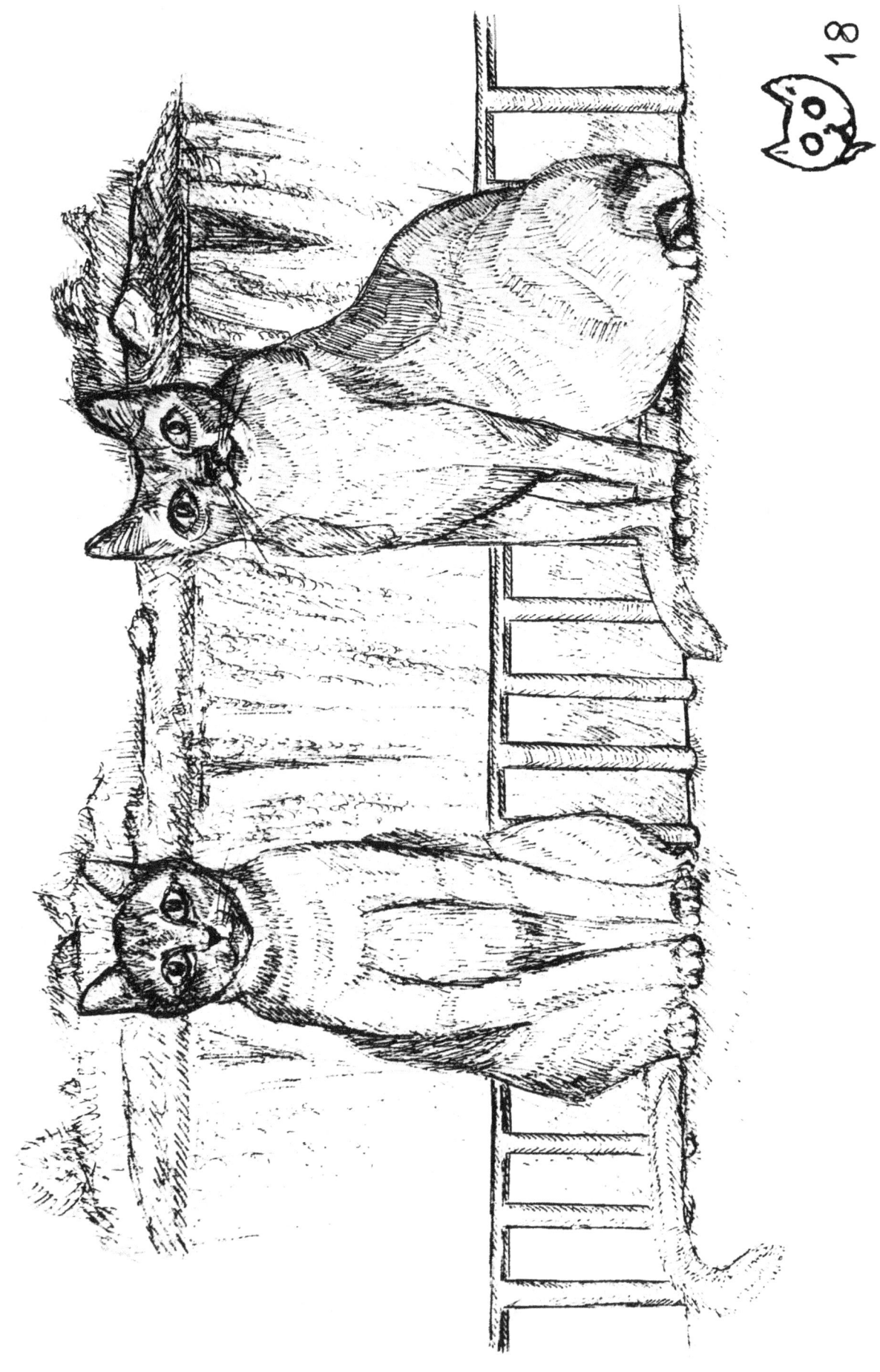

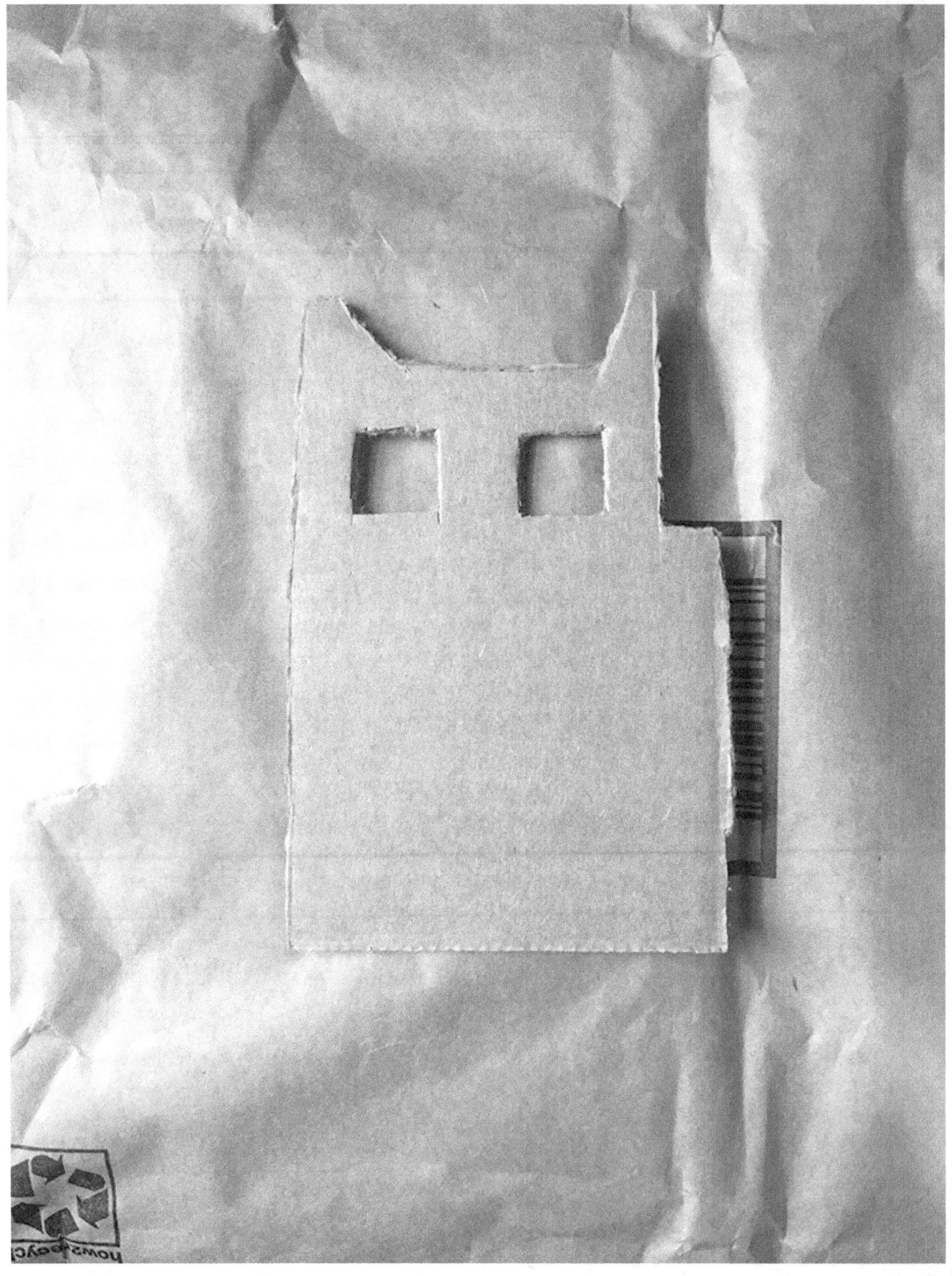

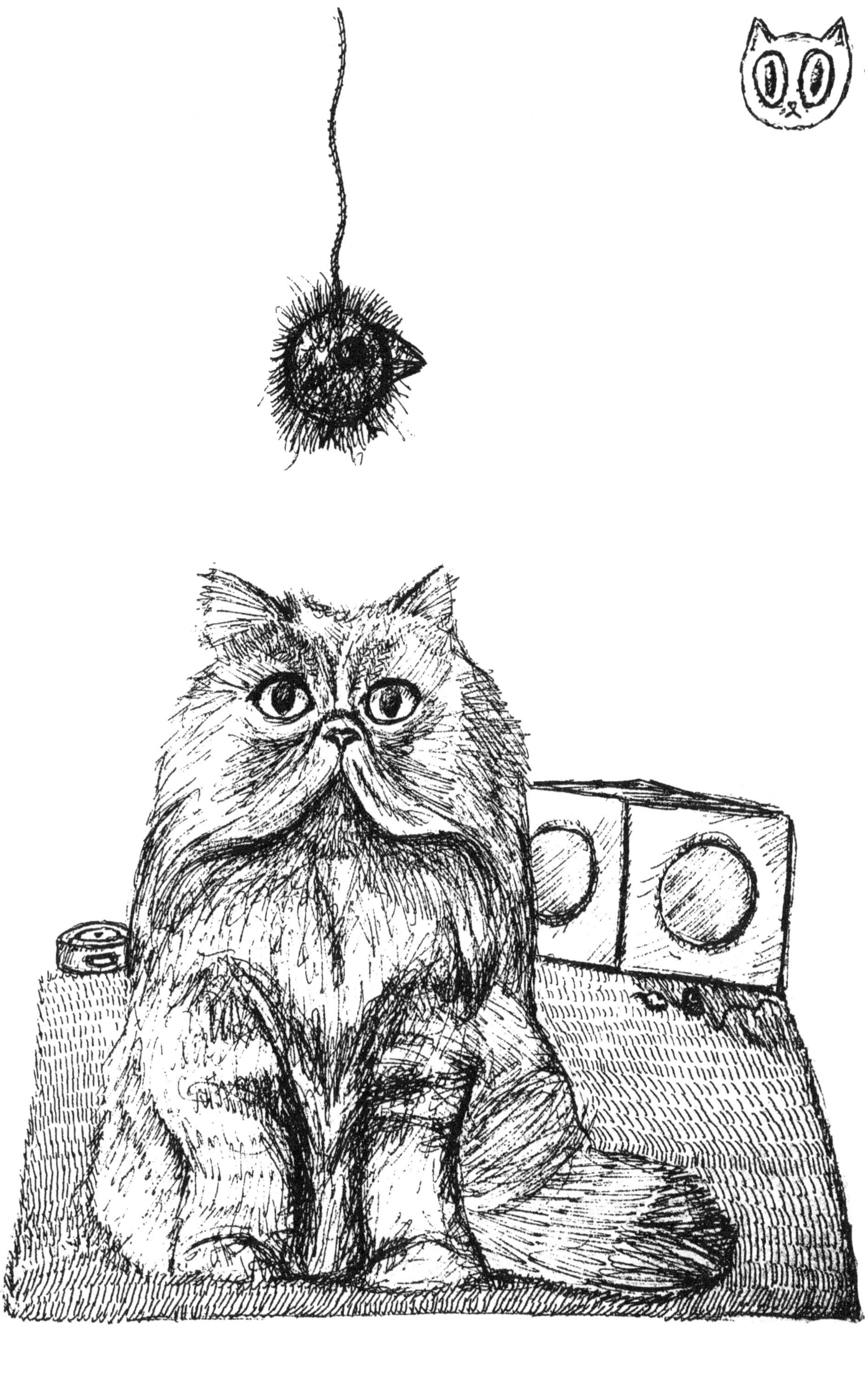

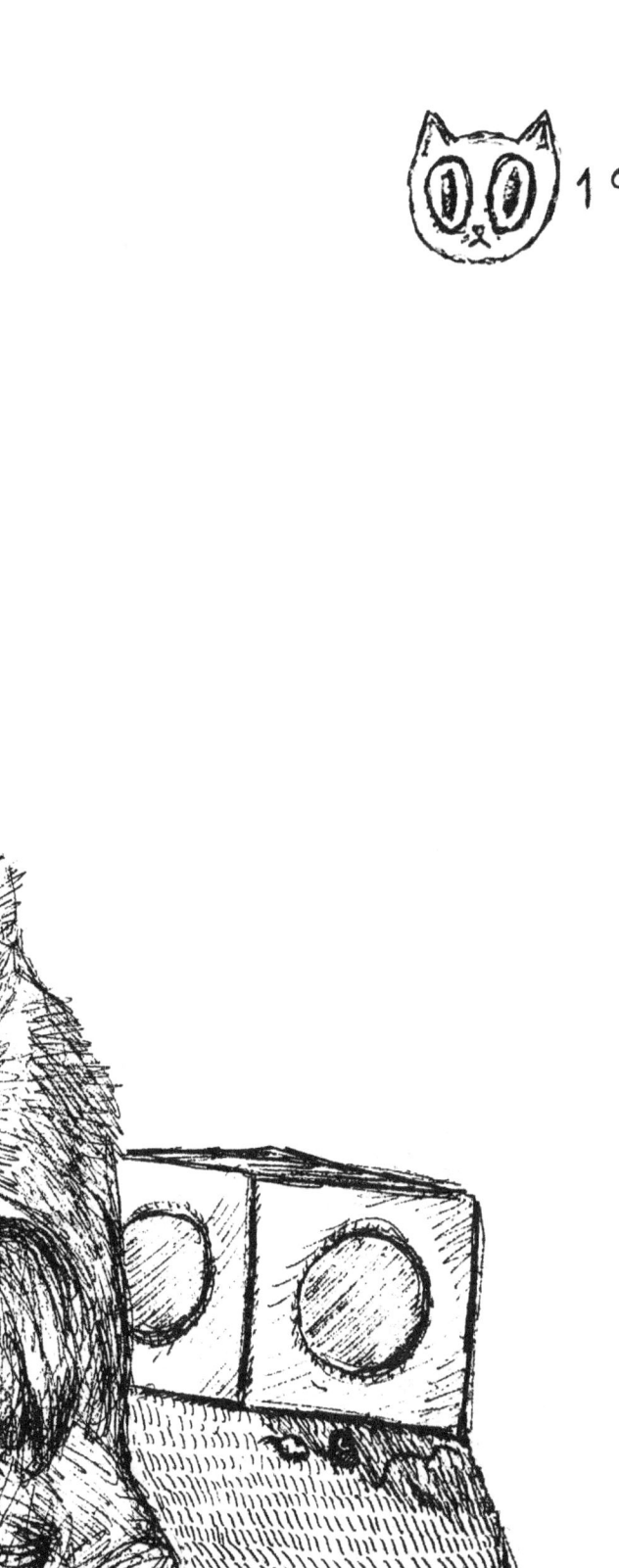

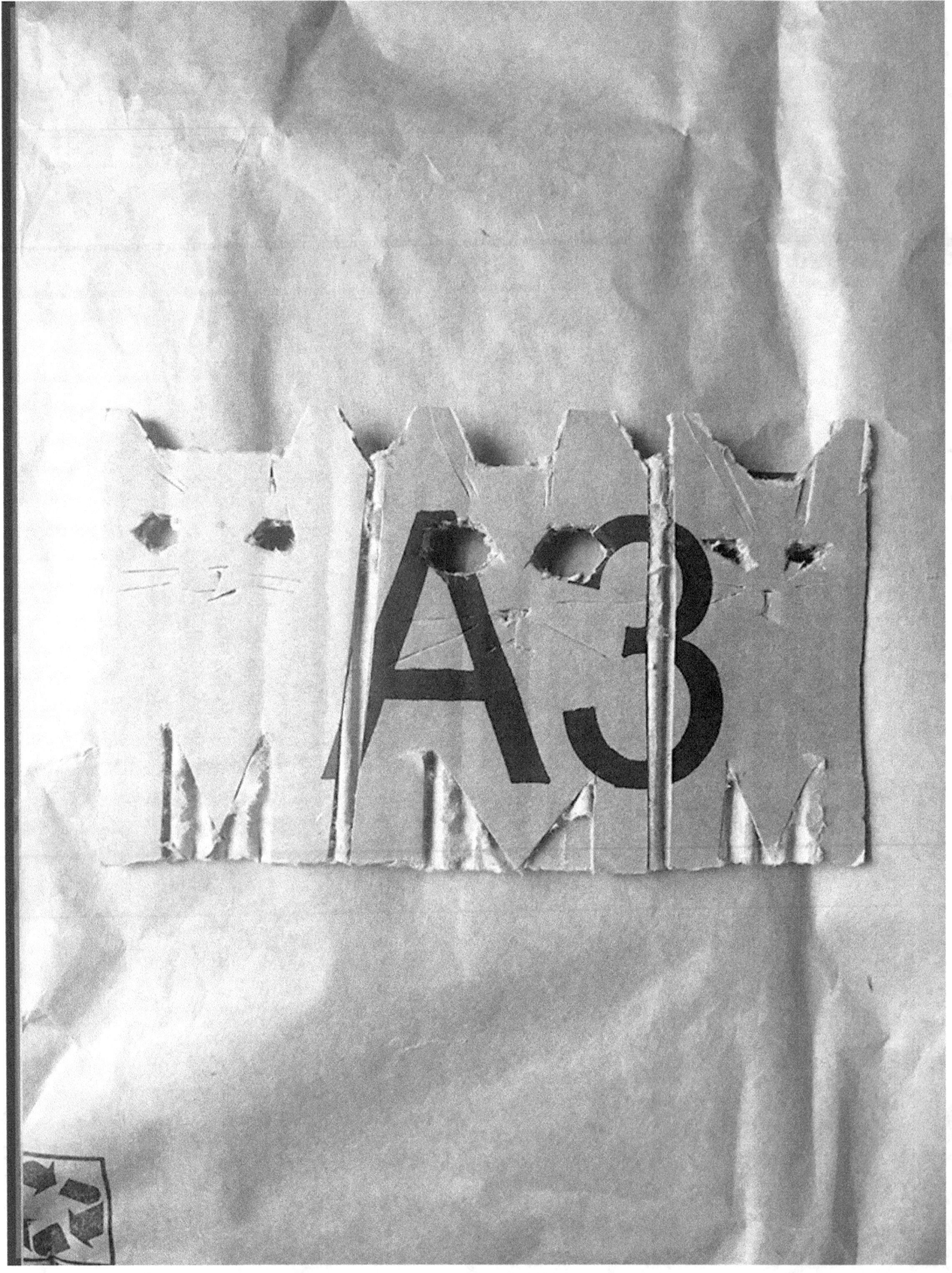

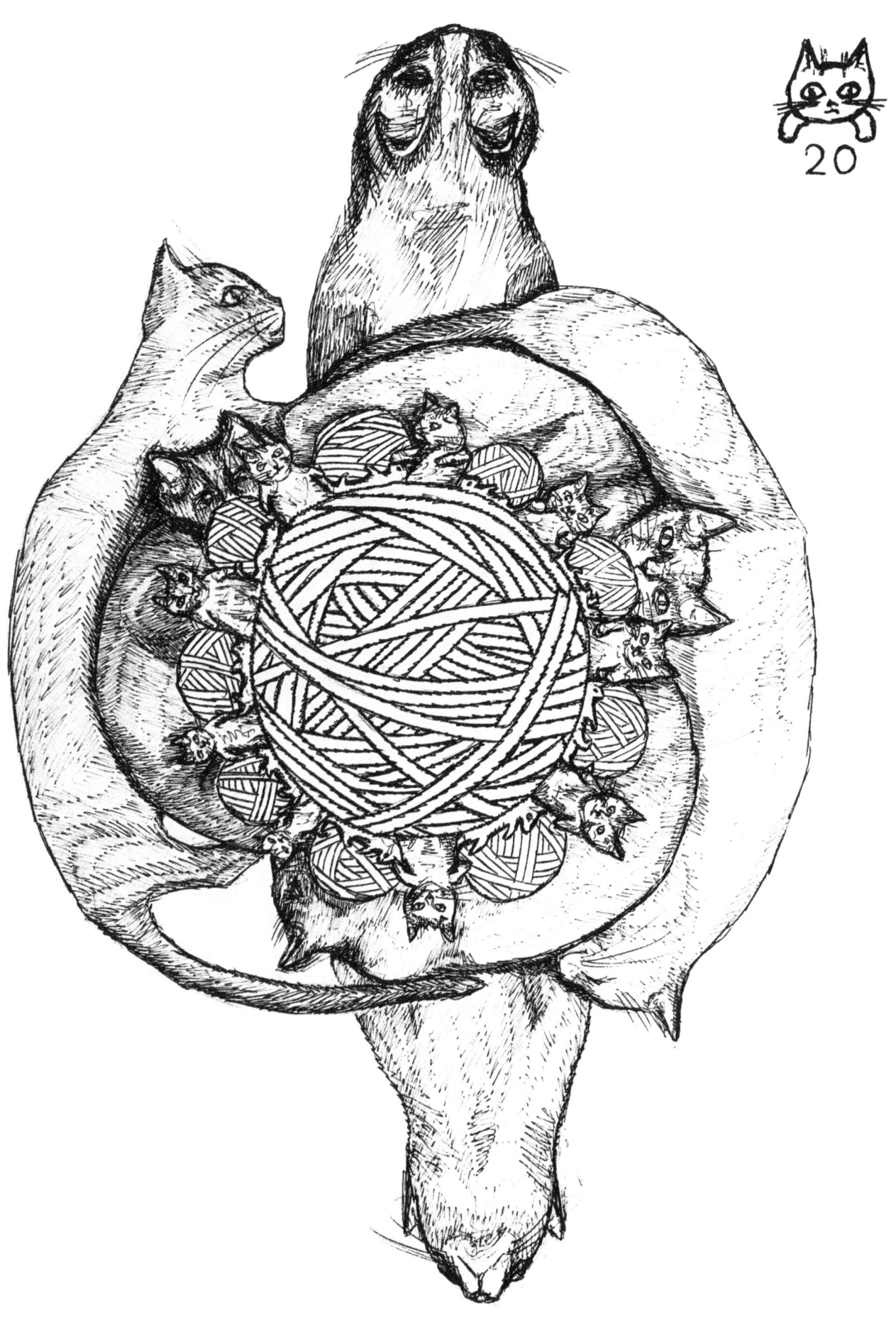

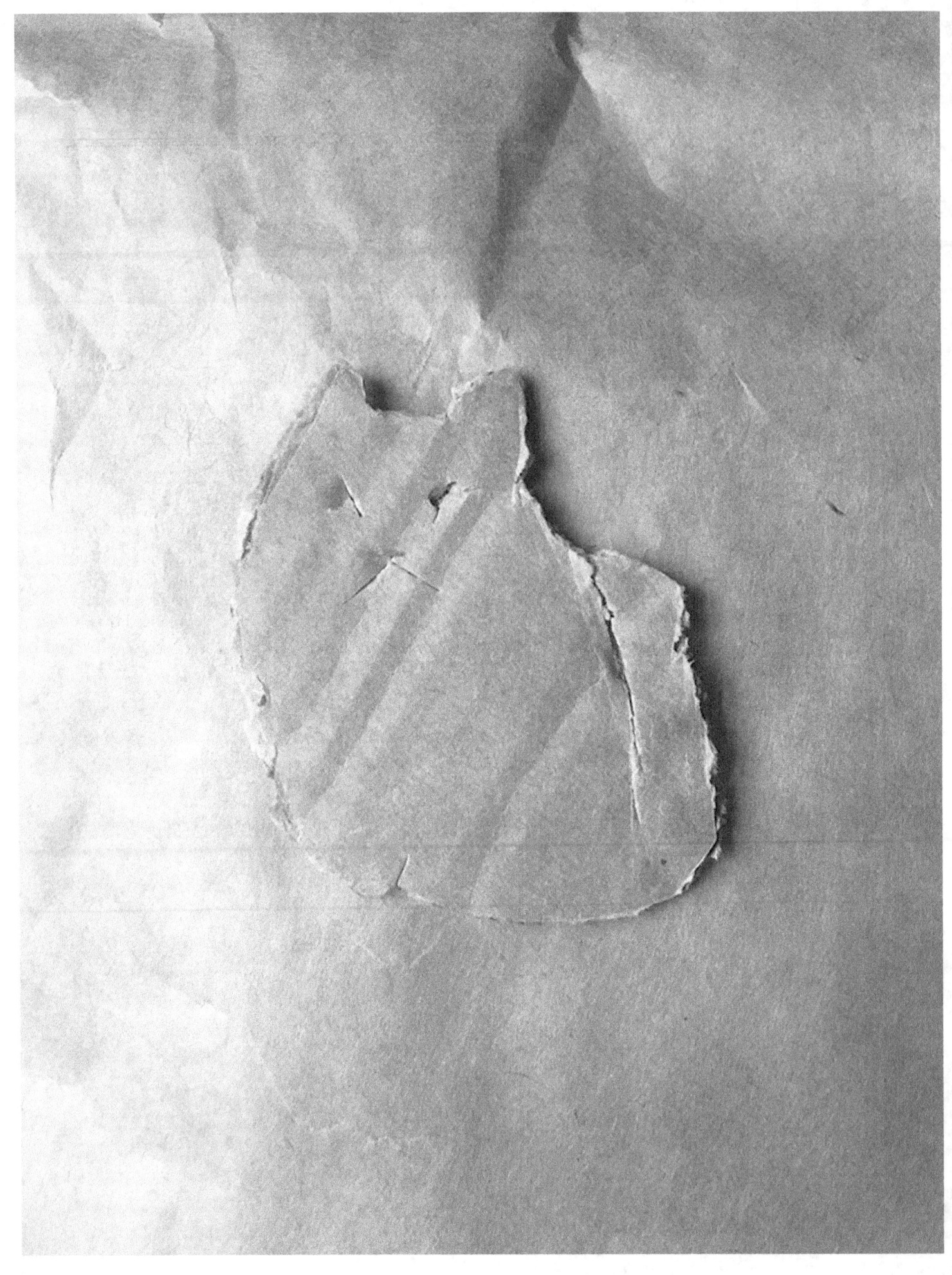

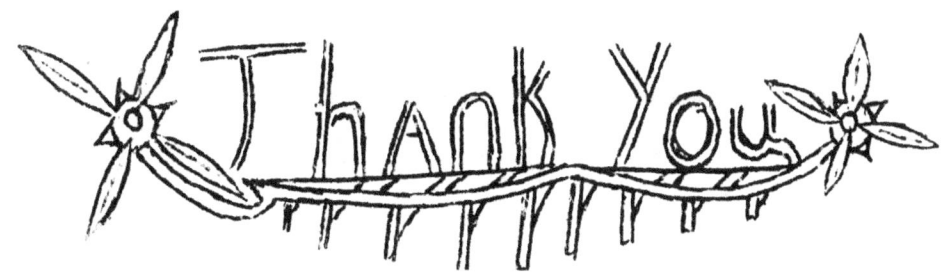

I hope you enjoyed this book!

If you want to see more, or want to know of any future books or work by aux you can find me from my website

auxdesigns.wordpress.com

I would love to see your results! ^.^

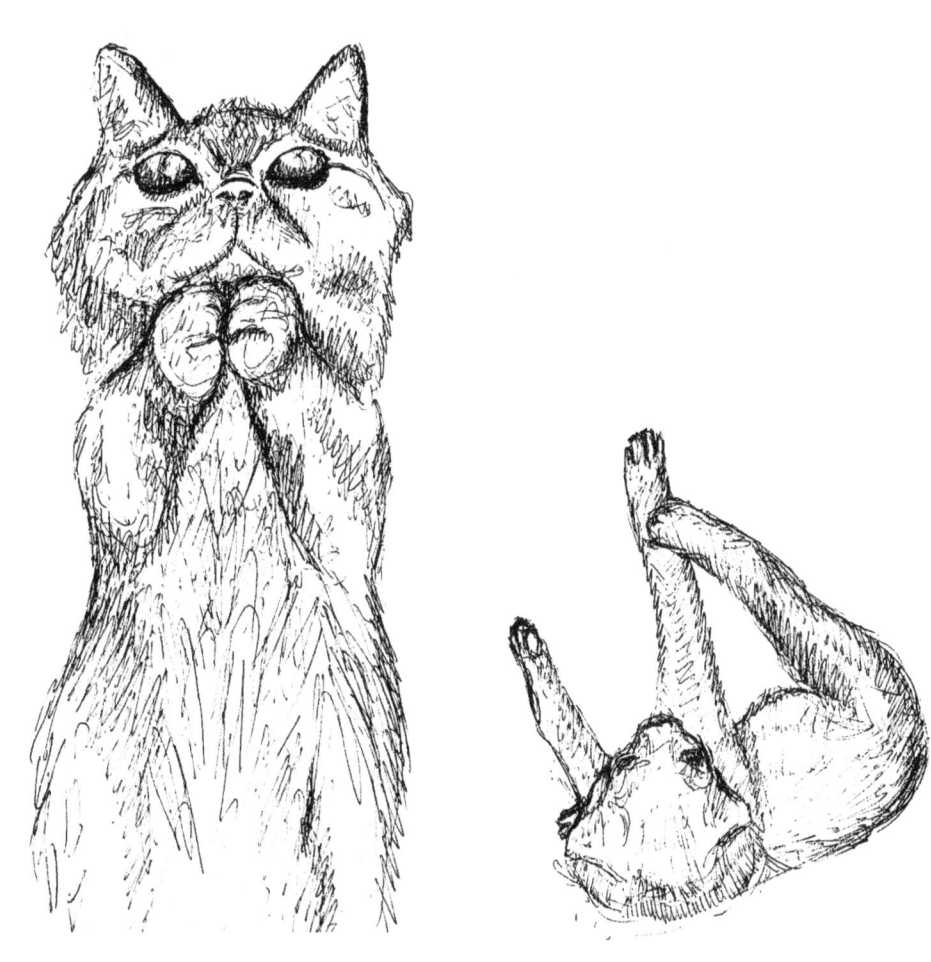

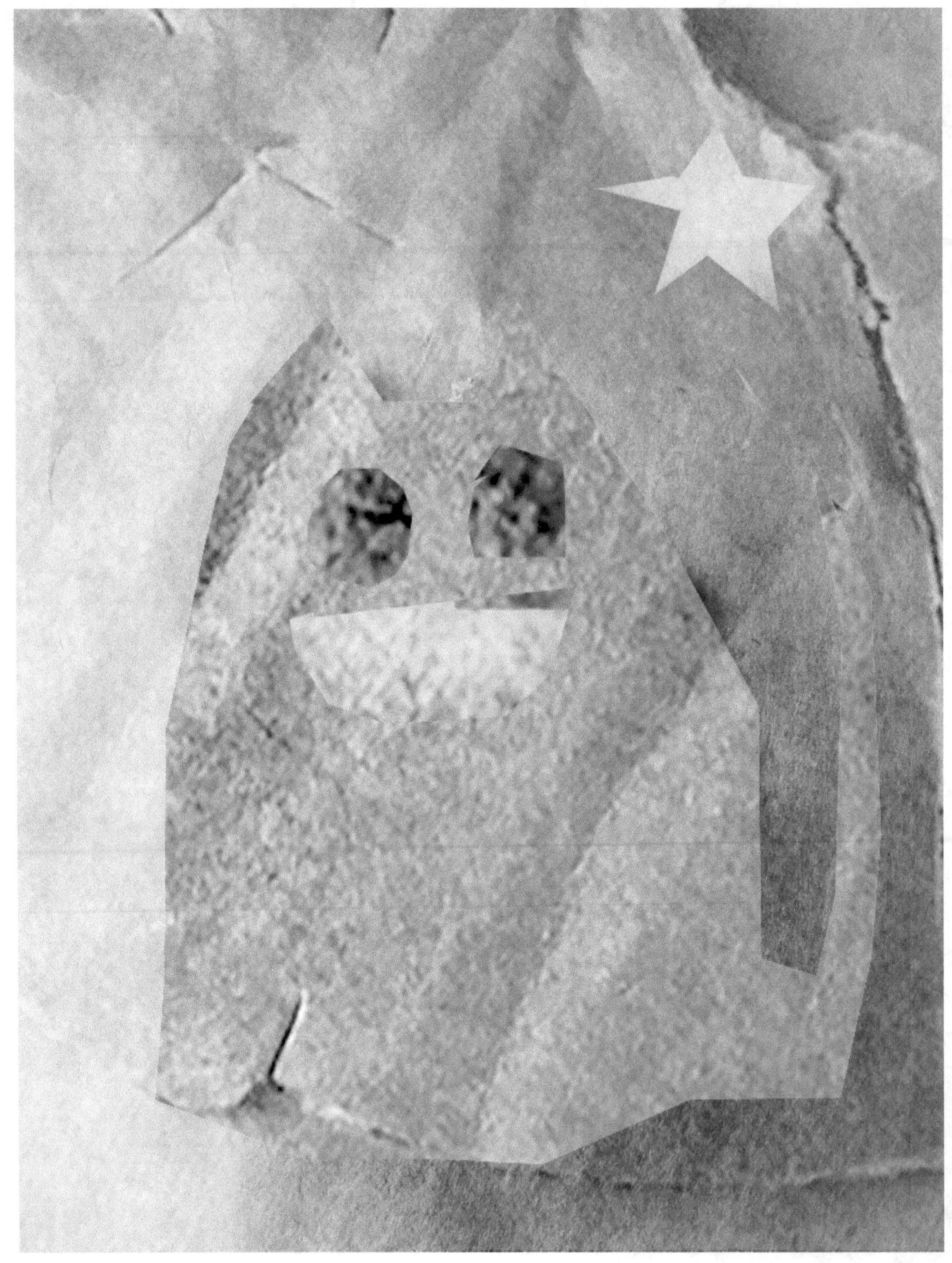

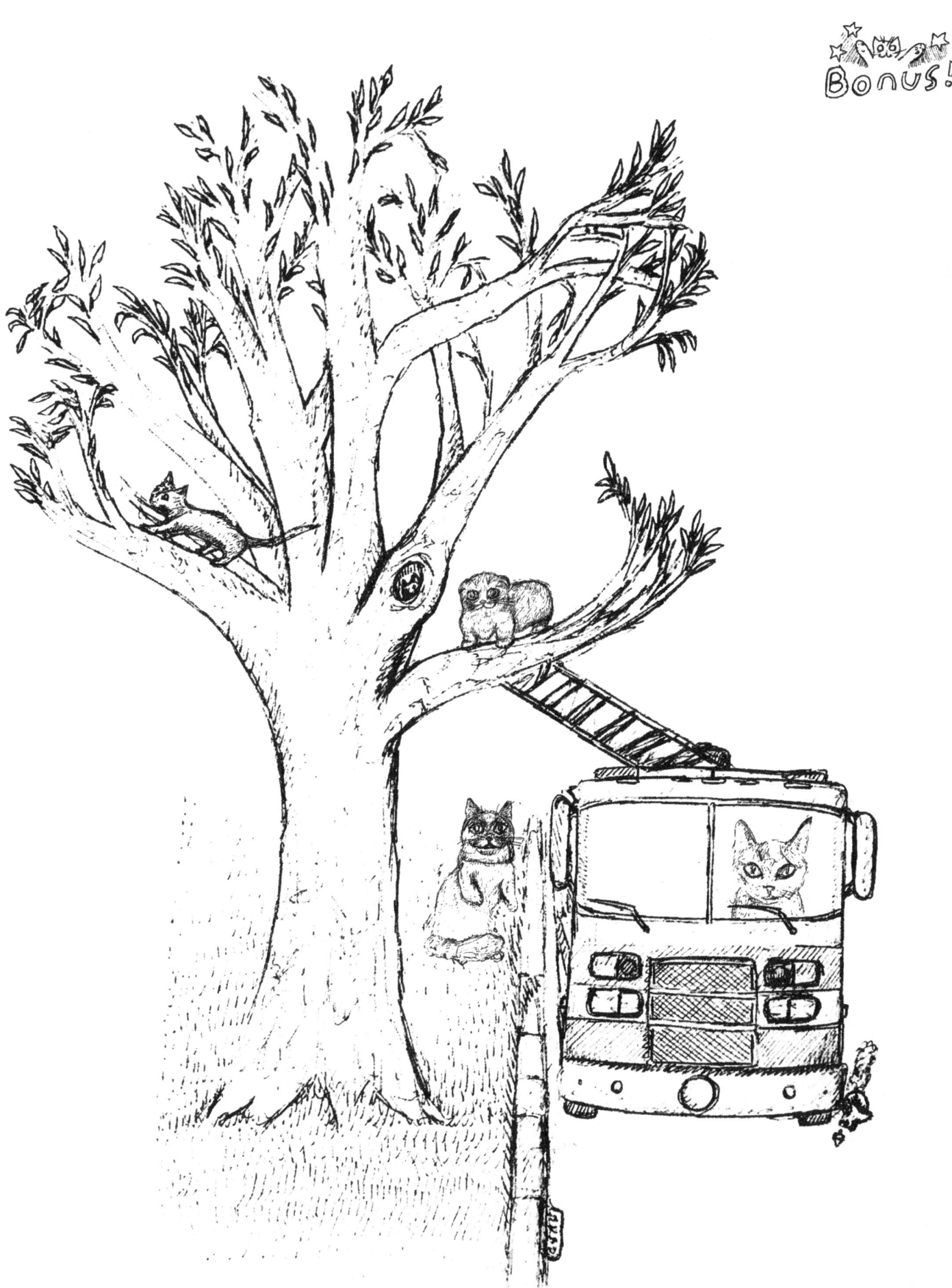

Bonus!